AF673690

> You begin saving the world by saving one person at a time; all else is grandiose romanticism or politics.
>
> — Charles Bukowski

Warm Loving Medication

AKSHAT SRIVASTAVA

KHANNA PUBLISHING HOUSE

Price: ₹ 299.00

Warm Loving Medication

***by* Akshat Srivastava**

Copyright © Author

This book has been published in good faith that the material provided by author is original. Every effort is made to ensure accuracy of material, but publisher and printer will not be held responsible for any inadvertent errors. In case of any dispute, all legal matters to be settled under Delhi jurisdiction only.

This book is sold subject to the condition that it shall not, by way of trade or otherwise, be lent, resold, hired out, or otherwise circulated without the publisher's prior consent in any form of binding or cover other than that in which it is published and without a similar condition including this condition being imposed on the subsequent purchaser and without limiting the rights under copyright reserved above, no part of this publication may be reproduced, stored in or introduced into retrieval system, or transmitted any form or by any means (electronic, mechanical, photocopying, recording or otherwise), without the prior written permission of both the copyright owner and the above mentioned publisher of this book.

ISBN: 978-93-89139-09-9

First Edition: 2020

Published by:

KHANNA PUBLISHING HOUSE
4C/4344, Ansari Road, Darya Ganj, New Delhi-110 002
Phone: 011-23244447-48 Mobile: +91-9910909320
E-mail: contact@khannabooks.com

Printed in India by:
S.P.S. Printers & Binders, Delhi

Contents

Preface

Characters in this novel are drawn from real life. Some from mine and others from the strangers we meet. Stories are observations with life, too. Meera is the one woman in everyone's life. The one woman who pushes them to do their best just to realise that sometimes our best isn't enough. Abir is the same man we always have been. Balanced, confused, drunk on love and shame. These stories are seen everywhere. You can see a part of them in your life or a loved one's just the same. The divine comedy that we call love and misery is that they are the biggest cliché. It hits you like a drunk Mike Tyson would if you accidentally flirted with his girl. Probably worse. I wouldn't know. There are multiple complications that I've faced with our people. There are those who care too much and there are those who do it too little. We have all been that person. Blessed are those who do it just the right amount. Loving too much becomes obsession and loving someone not as much as you could is a crime. We are all impatient creatures. We want everything too soon. Either we get it on our own terms or we do not want it at all. If we don't get what we want once, we tend to believe that we won't get anything that we want. But if you really ask yourself, a piece of you would always want to be more affectionate like you were as a kid. We adults are left with trust issues, unrequited love, traumas, fears, illness and experiences that are beyond any comprehension. As we grow up, every part of us wants us to drift away from the trust and love we once had for everyone. We do it in the name of wisdom. We do it in the name of maturity. It's a shame how people seldom love more in the name of wisdom anymore. People never let their guards down. They don't have as much to lose as they think they would. No one does. I did not.

I wouldn't judge the people who do have a lot to lose. I would be a tiny bit jealous of them to be honest. I would wish them the best and be happy that they're happy. It's something about this age that we are living in. We are not too old to have real responsibilities and we are not young enough to have none at all. This all started after someone I met decided to kill herself. Half of the people blamed her for being weak. The other half was too busy finding faults in her lifestyle. She was seen as lazy, weak, dumb and irresponsible. Some people even went on to question her character. Portraying her family as victims of the vicious acts of the underage daughter. But what else do you expect from a society that expects more accountability from students who protest, than they do from people who are abusing their powers on a daily basis. The more I think about the world, the more I want to stay alone. If you've felt like I do, you always need a Siddharth in your life. A friend who stays around you a lot. You need parents who accept who you are and give you the space you need. Most of all you need a Meera. Someone who makes you want to stay. Who makes you fall in love with the world again. Meera doesn't make you feel like you're alone in the kindness you carry like mountains on your shoulders. You always need a Meera to show you that you are everything and nothing. Most of all you need a Meera to figure out that you don't have to be unhappy. That you can be loved. Everyone can be loved, to be honest. Rarely are people loved the way they want to be loved. It is weird how so many crimes are done in the name of love. Riots in the name of people's love for their God. Men throwing acid at women they "love" after they don't show the same interest. Parents smothering their children. People are abused by their spouse in the name of affection. Men and Women held captive by each other's arms tied around their neck. Arms that turn into collars that are held by a leash called loneliness. I have been held captive by the same leash and I have held other people with the same.

The funny thing about falling in love is that it breaks you and if you do it right, rebuilds you into someone else. Someone you've always wanted to be. There are so many things you put on hold in your life until someone comes along and tells you don't have to. You can be anything to you want to be. They help you become the person you want to be. Some people are lucky to have a lot of people do the same for them. Some are unlucky enough to not have even one. They can do things to you that you could not comprehend. They could turn an atheist into a religious freak. They could turn a workaholic quit their job to go searching for something you would call a soul. There's nothing you could do when it hits you. You just get swayed and find yourself desperate like you've never been. You find yourself crying when you didn't know you had to. You find yourself looking at them and finding out that they're everything you want. And at one point you might have to accept that you can't have everything you want. Everyone doesn't get what's due. If everyone were with who they wanted to be with, the world would be a big open relationship.

Another thing about love and loss is that it comes at the right time like it should. For some people it doesn't leave. They are blessed. For people like us, all we can do is learn what we can and build a beautiful life. A life that we deserve. It is never too late to do it. We should be kinder to other people but more so to ourselves. If I had to ask something of you, I would ask you to be a bit more patient. Life will take you where you're supposed to be. It always does.

Let me finish this off a story I love.

There was a kid who used to play out fantasies in real life. Sometimes he'd be a fireman, another he'd be a policeman and so on. His parents saw that as a dysfunction so they took him to a therapist.

"I think he has multiple personality disorder and mild Bipolar disorder." said the therapist.

"What do we do Doctor?" The parents were desperate.

"He just needs warm loving..." continued the doctor.

"Warm Loving Care?" he was interrupted by the concerned parents.

"Medication. Warm Loving Medication." The doctor started writing a prescription, "Heavy medication."

Akshat Srivastava

Long Lost Bliss

Everyone I have met has a story to tell to a certain extent. Some of these stories can be melancholically beautiful, some a fucking travesty and some just happy go lucky. The ones I hate most are happy go lucky stories. Why? The main reason being most of the people who are happy are not thinking about their lives. My thought process runs in a singular direction: If you don't like something, change it. Most people who are happy without any reason are not thinking about what's wrong. If you don't know what's wrong, how do you fix it? For example, if Vincent Van Gogh wasn't diagnosed for his *schrizophoenia*, *depression* and *anxiety* and he didn't take the medication he was prescribed, would we have the poetic colourful masterpieces that we do? If you read about it, his medication made him feel the colour "yellow" a bit more than usual. That's why he painted the sunflowers or the bright light monstrosity of stars in his painting "The starry night." What if Kurt Cobain didn't snort the amount of cocaine that made Mia Wallace OD? Would we have the Nihilistic masterpieces that defined an era? That's why I have a habit of letting things flow. You need to have a zeal that lets you do what comes to mind. It's also a privilege to be afford this particular zeal. Maybe the worst of fires forge the mightiest of swords, who knows?

The current scenario of my life is emotionally exhilarating, physically demeaning and spiritually liberating. A friend messaged me today. A friend I had met years ago. A friend who made me cry on a long drive. Rehan. I met Rehan in a train ride to Kota. He's been a friend ever since. Kota is a place like no other. It is the right mix of smoking teens, sexual freaks, motivated jerks and the crippling lack of motivation in me. The whole time in Kota sent me into a downward spiral.

I agreed to investing my time there, too. Why? You can't just let someone who's been there all your life, had made sacrifices for you in the extremities, down. I couldn't do that to my parents. I wasn't strong enough. I didn't know what I wanted if not that. So I shipped off to Kota to try to be a better man in the only scale I had known. Zero exposure is more toxic than a bucket-full of HIV. Being at the wrong place at the wrong time destroys your spirit. That's what happened. My time there was much like a horror movie. From suicides here and there, to hearing voices that were supposed to be in my head. Not eating or sleeping for days does that to you, maybe. What interested me most about Kota was whenever I'd go on a run, all I would see was kids smoking cigarettes with their girlfriends. I didn't smoke then and peer pressure was the last thing that could affect me. The only pressure I take is of my morality. Which is pretty flawed and downright retarded. Kota, without doubt was the darkest period of my life. Tearing me away from the only thing I loved, art. There were nights I'd want to die. There were days I wouldn't want to see. There were interested girls I wouldn't want to see, let alone fuck. I had no spirit left. Every night, I'd go to the terrace of my hostel which was a nightmare. I'd pull up a chair and just look at the moon. A few months later, Rehan shifted his hostel to mine. I was the only friend he had. He was the only one I did.

So, one night after months of heavy depression, tight insomnia and mild schizophoenia what made me cry was Rehan's story. Rehan came from Srinagar. If you're unfamiliar with the situation of Kashmir, being an Indian, I wouldn't like you as a person. The only thing I hate is ignorance.

Ignorance brings hate, hate bring injustice and injustice crushes the brave hearts of kind people. It's a vicious circle. Rehan never had a family. He was brought up by his Aunt who lived alone after the death of everyone in their family. They dies in a bombing. It reminded me of a time when I was in Kashmir and my friends and I'd discuss bombings in our school just for fun. As kids we didn't know the value of lives that were at stake. We couldn't comprehend a death and the loss it could bring to hundreds. Rehan lost seven family members in a blast at Lal Chowk. He then went on to be a strong individual who lived a beautiful life by his own measures. He then went on to lose his aunt about an year before we met. He had a story to share. I wanted to hear it.

"When I was in seventh grade, I met Mumtaz. I used to be bullied by the kids in school, so she'd come sit with me. No one wants to bully a kid in-front of a girl. It's funny how people's morality and actions, change when they want to please someone. Mumtaz and I, grew up together and had a beautiful life. Naturally, we fell in love. She loved the way I sketched, I loved the way she made everything feel beautiful enough to sketch. She loved the way I sang, I loved the way she listened to me. I loved the way she'd keep her Pashmina on her head when it was very cold and she loved the way I made Kahwah for her. There was a feeling in my head, a feeling I could always comprehend but could never feel. She made me feel that indescribable feeling. That feeling only once you've had it, you'll realise you've always wanted it. The first time I saw her, she was adjusting a Pashmina Shawl over her head because it had suddenly started snowing. It's beautiful how it would snow randomly in Kashmir. That was the first sketch of her, that I made. I showed it to her years later when we knew we wanted each other. I still remember the tear in her eyes. It was also the last time I had seen her. Quite an image to carry. I wish the last time I saw her, I could've made her snort like my cute little piggy like she was. It's funny how us guys see a lot of things before falling in love and some women just look at your face with the eyes of utter adoration and absolute beauty. It doesn't matter to them if you look like a rotten tomato having a bad day, if they love you they'll look at you as if someone looked at their God….."

"For the last time? Before you came to Kota?" I interrupted him like the ignorant idiot I was.

"No, my friend. It was a couple of years ago." He said looking down. His eyebrows were tight. His lips sealed shut.

"Why? What happened?"

"What always happens to me… I love someone. I make a home with them. They die. It's difficult not to see a pattern, you know. How someone I love, dies."

"She died? How?" I almost spat out the tea I was sipping.

"There was a protest against army rule at Lal Chowk. Like every other empathetic person, she was a bit into protesting for what felt right. I was about to go with her but my aunt was sick. So, I couldn't. A few days later I went to her place, only to get the news. There was a bombing at Lal Chowk that day. That lead to a stampede. That's how it ended for her."

"How do you keep on living with it? I cannot comprehend the extent of pain you went through. The only reason I don't do it is because the pain it'd bring to my parents. What's stopping you?" I asked a stupid question out of an ignorant mind.

"It's simple. The only reason to live is life. Life is supposed to be lived. Everything will work out someday. I promised her that I'd live no matter what. I intend to keep that promise."

When my friend texted me today, I was smoking a cigarette just like that unfortunate night. I told him, I now understand the feeling that I had always wanted, the feeling that came to me in the form of Meera and then that feeling left.

"I have my first fine art exhibition at the India Habitat Centre in Delhi on 27th of March. If you don't come to my exhibition, I will visit Patiala. I have a painting for you." Rehan told me.

"Obviously, I'll be there. I gotta tell you something. I am getting a book published. It's about everything and nothing. I can't describe it. I'll email you the first draft if you wanna read."

"Did you write the book when you had her or when you didn't anymore?"

"I had half of my book when I was with her. I had stopped writing because I was happy in a long-long time. I finally had a home."

"Maybe the beauty of that feeling is that it doesn't last. Maybe the reason of that feeling is so that pain can bring you closer to your destiny. If they didn't leave, I wouldn't have my exhibition and you wouldn't have your book."

"Man, I'd give up a thousand books for her." I laughed.

"If only that trade was possible.." His voice turned coarse..

There was a time when I wouldn't understand what was feeling that made you love something or someone beyond your present comprehension. There was a time when I wanted to understand things I couldn't. There was a time I wandered because nowhere felt like home. It still doesn't. It's okay to be scared of love, it's okay to run away from it. When love comes, it doesn't plead. Love commands. Love dictates. That was the first night I smoked a cigarette.

Why? Just like life is supposed to be lived. A cigarette is supposed to be smoked and a tear is supposed to be shed. A laugh is supposed to be laughed and a heart is supposed to be full of love. If not for a person, then for the world. Love doesn't hurt. Envy hurts. Insecurity hurts. Disapproval hurts. Betrayal hurts. The only thing that keeps us going is love.

•••

The Flight

Like majority airlines in this world, this particular airlines had a habit of pissing me off too. Maybe because I never liked flights. Flights feel like Purgatory, you're neither happy nor you're sad. Your ears sort of hurt and yet they don't. You are breathing artificial air that sort of makes you want to die a bit. Infants and toddlers would cry and most of the people just want to reach their destination without dying.

Although there are all kinds of reasons to hate flights, the main reason why I despise flying is how people try to be better when they enter a flight. Like they weren't all that great before they could be graced by an airline in their lives. Everyone utilises all their energy and wit being someone they are not but they'd rather be. Bachelors are all about joining the mile high club. Elderly are mostly very disrespectful to the hospitality team of any establishment. Amusing because it is the only place I see good looking people being treated badly without any particular reason. What pisses me off the most is how the managers at these establishments would treat their own people. They would push their own people overboard to keep the ship floating. That's hospitality for you. Don't hate the player, hate the game.

Now to fuel the fire of my perpetual mid-air agony, on that special occasion I had contacted a throat infection. So I couldn't speak, and my ears rang louder than all the bells in Vatican. I boarded this specific flight back from Goa. Since, I couldn't listen to music I utilised my time to edit some portraits I had clicked for a client on commission. I was letting out sighs of disappointment at the pictures I had to click so as to please a client. I needed inspiration. I just wanted to throw my camera at someone's head, thanks to the kinds of clients I was getting these days. Who knows what would happen if all the people of the world would stop doing what they love for inspiration? That's freelancing for you.

There are always a few moments in your life that are very unpredictable. You end up doing something that you'd never dream of doing and end up in a scenario which you could've never imagined being in. Something was going to happen that would change everything I ever believed in. Amid these strangers who were either happy after a holiday high or were sad because they were going to their usual lives, I saw someone who drew my attention immediately. The head of the cabin crew, she was a tall woman with short Mia Wallace hair. Althrough, the appealing aesthetic nature of her face all I could see was that she had a very strong expression on her face with incredibly sad eyes. People like that usually gain my attention very quickly. There is a story behind them that needs to be heard.

The next thing I knew, the in-flight services had begun. I wish one of these services was being thrown out of flight. The cart pulled up right next to me. There she was. The object of my curiosity. She looked at me with a blank face.

'Sir, have you travelled with us before? Maybe on our last flight from Delhi?" asked the uniformed mystery with a blank face as any professional would.

"Hell nah. I don't think so. I think I would've remembered you." I said in my head. Wise choice not to say that out loud.

But I chose to be civil and raised my shoulders in an awkward fashion to suggest the crippling uncertainty. Decent way to start a conversation, wouldn't you think?

In the glance, that we shared right there and then, my curiosity for her had reached the roof. It was hard to keep a lid on it. Well, during that flight whenever I would look up there she was with a slight rightly timed eye contact and some shared awkwardness so as to why this was happening. I knew it was all pure coincidence.

I do believe that there is always a story being pulled towards me because of the natural need for it to be heard. I am not a story-teller, I am merely someone who loves listening.

Whenever I looked at her and we shared a glance, I got conscious. Why? Obviously, the main reason I didn't want to intimidate a girl just doing her job. Also, I didn't want to be a creep on a flight. I guess, there are plenty of those. So, I decided to take a step back. It's a difficult job, right? It's heartbreaking to see people working so hard to be treated like shit by any passenger who may not have even amounted to anything in their lives. People lie when they say money doesnt buy you happiness. It buys you people's silence in the face of disrespect. That is happiness to a lot of people.

What I did was the exact opposite of what my thought process would advise me. Here came a wonderful moment of my short life. I typed a message in the notes app of my phone. The message was all over the place.

It said, "I think you are beautiful. I would love to photograph you and publish it if the results came out appealing. You have this Mia Wallace hair and it is drawing me to you. I could photograph you right here if it's okay."

When I handed her that phone I had a strong feeling that hell is coming my way but to the contrary she smiled and she was actually amazing about the whole thing to my surprise. That was the first time in the whole flight I saw her smile and hell did come my way.

"Well we aren't allowed to get photographed in our uniform especially not in flights." She said. Another reason for me to sigh and think, "Fuck flights."

"How about you give me a way to contact you, so that you can see my work and decide if you want to go through with this?"

She already had my phone in her hand and she gave me her details. I was happy I guess. I don't remember the last time I was happy without a reason. The last time probably when I joined my job as a business analyst. I am someone who used to be really optimistic but now hands down nihilistic. So I try to avoid getting excited for anything. So finally I slept at 4 am the same time I always do in this amazing life of mine. I don't remember what I had in my mind, it was either excitement or throat pain.

Being a curious soul I was, I stalked her social media. There were a lot of pictures of her with a kid and I thought it was her daughter. It somehow felt like an evil thing, how attracted I was to a mother. It didn't bother me much, considering how astonishingly beautiful she was to my eyes. How in all her pictures she looked so happy and lively but the last time I saw her in person, she had the saddest eyes I had ever seen. The way we try to be happy for social media will always be overwhelming to me.

"Heyy." I texted her.

"Heyy." She replied.

Somehow, I had a feeling it was the beginning of something. Something troublesome maybe but beautiful regardless.

•••

Meera

With people I have only one rule: All you can know about a person is what they choose to share with you. The rest is just a story you build in your pretty little head. Loving someone is just taking a chance. Taking a leap of faith. There is a thing about leap of faiths, either you survive and have something beautiful in your matured hands or you die with a broken neck. Similar to most creatures life is unpredictable to the people who don't think about it. Sometimes, as a kid you could never predict who you would be when you were twenty. As a kid, it is easier. Everyone is a friend, everyone wants to play, everyone is hopeful in life. I guess as people grow older they grow less mature. Fighting about things they want and can't get. What's funny is as kids we would fight for toys or burgers or other things. As an adult we fight for things that are out of our control. A job, a woman's love, a lot of us even fight for appreciation and approval from people we probably won't ever talk to again. I've known people who've spent all their lives trying to please everyone around them, which usually puts your life in the hands of others. There is a difference between being selfish and cautious.

It was just a usual morning, I was in a cab that was headed towards the office I loved. Why did I love that office? I worked in a startup. In my young ignorance it was easy to believe how it was a friendly environment. There were a few people whom I could trust with my heart and soul. It was mostly how I looked forward to seeing them, working with them and at the end of the day sharing a joint with them. Like most managers, my manager was a hard-ass. He was good at his job, he shaped people into good working professionals but I was just too stubborn to be one. There was a general dislike directed towards him around the office because he felt like a corporate manager in a startup culture. Almost as if both of us didn't belong there. That same evening, I had a date planned with a girl I knew a few years ago. I had a huge crush on her but I wasn't hot enough back then. I wasn't hot enough now, either. I somehow just knew how to push the right buttons.

That morning was different. On a usual cab trip, I would mostly either sleep or listen to some motivational music. Looking out of the window, I saw the Delhi roads filled with cars in a standstill with time itself. It was a limbo. My cab driver was blasting some Punjabi song about cars, dames and money. Classic. I put my earphones on and started playing some classic jazz. The vibe was different somehow that day. As soon as I put on the playlist, a notification popped up on my phone. I thought it would be the same office group notifying each other about our whereabouts. I checked it with the general indifference.

"Hey. I am in Kerala. What about you?" Meera had texted.

At this point of time, Kerala was heavily flooded. There were various NGOs and Applications giving every individual a chance to help out. Who was gonna believe NGOs run by the wives of money-mongering millionaires?

"What are you doing there? Isn't it flooded?" I asked her.

"Can I call you? I am barely receiving any data here." She replied.

"Sure sure." I replied acting cool but I was a kid smiling like the Joker in Batman Arkham Asylum.

As soon as she called me, she told me she was running a small service where she'd take donation from people around her and buy supplies with it. She'd then personally go and donate these supplies to the Armed Forces operating in that area.

For the first time in my short life, someone had surprised me. People our age group were either busy struggling with love, getting high off their minds or working in NGOs to secure certificates that would help them in reaching good B-schools. She broke the monotony. I wanted to donate too, so I told her if she needs any help.

"I'll skim you off of all your money as soon as I am back." She said in a childishly happy voice.

I'll never forget that voice.

It was these small things that were drawing me closer to her. As soon as she hung up, I called my date. I cancelled on her. Why? I wouldn't know. Maybe, because Meera was something else to me. I would rather not spend time chasing around someone I don't want. In a few days, Meera and I had planned a meeting. Obviously, it was all about clicking these pictures. I was a professional so I would never have the wrong intentions about it but somehow at the same time everything about her felt like it was pulling me to her. It felt amazing and at the same time it came with the promise of breaking my heart.

We decided to meet at CP, both of us were using the metro and we decided to meet a cafe coffee day inside the Rajiv Chowk Metro Station. She reached first and I was late. Not one of my finest qualities. I entered the coffee shop and I looked for her. I couldn't find her. Although, I did find a girl in a printed t-shirt with solid specs who looked different but similar. I realised one thing when I laid eyes on her, she looked super hot in her uniform and at the same time she was fucking absolutely breathtaking when she didn't even want to try.

We decided to go and sit somewhere at last. So we took to a usual restaurant and sat in a cliché setting. This whole time what was drew me to her most was how calm and composed she was. How she always had something logical to say amidst my fuckall rants. I got to know something about her, she was a grown up in so many ways while she was like a kid in many others.

She lost her parents when she was very young, which is heartbreaking. What really made it a big deal was that I could've never guessed looking at her that she went through such a trauma. Either she hid it pretty well or she was very good at recovering from traumas. At the same time, she had her flaws too but they don't matter as much as her qualities.

What really made a difference to me were the small things she said. Things she loved, the weird sparkle in her eyes that I hate, that she could simultaneously be a kid and one of the wisest people I've met. And I hang out with a lot of Old dudes. Old people love Abeer, as much as Meera hated walking. Like I said, there are a lot of people on this planet and some of them make life worthwhile for others. Some people just make the world a brighter place. They don't have to be activists or politicians or celebrities. All they could be is someone in the shadows (no matter what's going on in their head) trying to make the world better bit by bit.

Mostly, I have realised that people open up to me as fast as women would open their legs for Johhny Depp. Pop goes the weasel. In most cases, I would be the one sitting and listening. Here, it was different. I wanted to tell her about me. I wanted to tell her things I never told anyone else. I wanted to open every vein and let her see the real me but I didn't want to scare her off, so I didn't.

While talking to her, smoking a cigarette in that cafe. I broke my spectacles. My favourite goddamn glasses. It was a solid classic RayBan Wayfarer. I am not in materialistic things but this was the frame Rakeysh Omprakash Mehra was wearing when he signed my camera. (Yes, that happened.) I realised this after I left the bar. I couldn't find the handle but I was pretty sure I would find it if I had time. Time is what I didn't have. I was so engrossed in what she had to say and how I made her laugh I just let it be "Fuck the frame." I just continued indulging in her company. It was almost exciting. How natural it all was. So I did what any wise person would do. I chucked the handle, got my lenses transferred in a similar frame. What a pain in the ass that was.

She was worth all that and more. This woman was all that there was left in the world. Every other person, I knew had their heads so far up their asses of entitlement. The thing that would draw me to her most of time was the fact that she was sad. She was sad and she needed someone by her side and she was strong enough to be that person for herself. Weakness has a thing about it, it's a state of mind. Not being a victim, she was fighting her own battles while helping people and dodging assholes. If that is not admirable my friends, I don't know what is. She wasn't the victim that most people wanted to be. She was not someone who would want people to pamper her and take care of her. All she needed was someone to listen and all I wanted was to hear what she had to say.

•••

When Time Kept Pulling Us Towards Each Other

"I feel like I am about to die soon. The sad part is I am hoping I die soon. I am so tired of this world. My life has no meaning anymore. My friends have turned their backs on me because they feel like I give them a bad trip. Nothing means anything anymore," said Salim.

Who was Salim to signify the value of life you must think? Life's beautiful, right? Live. Laugh. Love. That's the motto our generation follows, right? It's actually a nice way to maintain the optimism in our lifestyles. So many people I've found in the dark hostel rooms of Kota who spend all their times either sleeping or binge watching shit they'd rather not watch if they were not in this predicament. There are hundreds of Internet Cafes in Kota that would transfer pirated movies or episodes of most TV series at fixed prices. There were so many businesses that were booming down there. Back when I was in Kota, I had a habit of going on a run everyday no matter what happened. I'd run even if it was raining and even if I had a fever. I'd go for runs after sunset because I hated days and evenings. Whenever you are in Kota, you should probably go to a few parks. In each park, most kids would be sitting around smoking cigarettes, making out with their girlfriends or just killing time in general. Let's say ninety percent of them. The kids who studied didn't even bother coming out in the evenings. Why was that these kids didn't see a future? Why did time stand still in a place that was filled with at least a quarter million kids each year? I don't have the answer to that either. I wish I did.

Salim was not from Kota. He was an engineer who was working as a business analyst in Gurugram. He had a "beautiful" family. He had a girlfriend. He earned copious amounts of money. Why was he calling a stranger on a suicide helpline? How could someone who built himself so well find himself to be so lonely that he had to ask a stranger for help? Fuck if I knew. All I could do was listen.

"I mean, it's almost like I feel people would be a lot happier if I wasn't around. I can't even tell my girl what I am going through. I am scared she'll have the same response as my friends." He continued. His voice choked.

It almost broke my heart to hear a twenty-eight year old someone talk the way he did. Is that what growing up feels like? Is that what happens? People you've known for years are just too busy to be there for you? Who knew?

"What would you want to change about your life? The things that you can control? You can't control other people's actions." I was curious.

It had been only a week since I started working there. I had no idea what I was doing. I was just an optimistic soul trying to help the world one person at a time.

"I would want to go back in time and change the path I've taken." He said.

"You can still take that path now." I told him.

"Maybe." He stopped crying.

"Just think about what you wanna change. I think the problem with us we expect too much from other people and not enough from ourselves." I didn't know what I was doing.

"I think so too." He was calm now.

"Can you just think about it once? What do you want with life? I truly believe things find their way once you become who you want to be." I told him.

"I'll think about it and call you tomorrow." His voice sounded optimistic.

He never called again. One can only assume if he killed himself or he worked towards a better life but one thing was for sure, he reached a conclusion. I can hope he chose life.

After that call ended, I fell on the sofa. It was late. I was exhausted. Emotionally and physically. It was killing me. My life these days was commuting to and from Gurugram, everyday. I lived in East Delhi. Three hours a day in a cab or Delhi metro. I wanted to move to Gurugram right there and then but whenever I'd talk about it my parents would seem extremely disappointed. The things we do for love. After that, I'd take some calls from the suicide helpline my friend started. Government suicide helplines worked, too. They worked like one of those South Delhi kids with Jaguars gifted to them by their rich ass parents. Rarely.

Like any millennial, at the end of the day I did what any smart person would do. I opened Facebook. Why? Memes. Memes and Vodka are the answer to life's problems. I opened my phone and there was a notification. These days, the only thing that would bring the widest of smiles on my face was the name Meera flashing on my phone.

"Landing in Delhi at 2 p.m. tomorrow." She had texted.

"Do you wanna get a drink in the evening?" I texted back.

"Maybe. I might be too exhausted." She replied.

"Come on. I'll get you alcohol." I smiled.

"Yasssss, I am boarding the flight now. I'll call you tomorrow." She replied.

As if I needed more reasons to hate flights. To all the Airlines that don't give the passengers and staff Wi-fi, fuck you.

We had met multiple times by now. Most of them, not so significant. Not significant for you, the world for me. It was a sheer pleasure being around that woman. Whenever we met we would go out to eat or something but we would just end up walking, talking, sitting and talking for really long periods. At this point it was so natural that it seemed more like we had known each other forever. We talked for most nights. Both of us suffered from Sleep Apnea. I think it was the only thing we had in common. We worked tirelessly and yet, we couldn't sleep. I had my reasons not to sleep. Given the significant number of mental illnesses I suffered from. What was her reason? Whatever it was, one thing was for certain. We brought each other happiness we couldn't find elsewhere.

Long story short, we met the next day. We hit a bar she recommended. A bar I'd never go to if not for her. I loved the fact that she was always in her nerdy t-shirts around me and I, in my most casual clothes. We didn't have to pretend. We didn't have to try. We just were who we were. Although I did wear boots most of the times because she was a bit taller than me and I was an insecure little bitch. Subconscious insecurity beats conscious insecurity any day. We had a few drinks.

"It's a shame that you're younger than me." Meera smirked.

Just as she said this, a bartender came and asked her for her ID. He wanted to check if she was legal drinking age. The legal drinking age in Delhi is twenty-five. I was twenty-two. She was twenty-seven. She immediately took out her ID and gave it to the bartender.

"Don't you need my ID?" I asked the bartender.

"Nah. You're fine." He asked me.

I laughed so hard. She was a bit embarrassed.

I turned to her.

"See? Age doesn't matter. Maturity does." I gave her a serious look. I believe I looked cool.

She laughed.

"Hey! Let's go watch this horror movie, Stree?" I suggested.

"Isn't it a bit late? It's 10 pm already. I have an early morning flight. Although, I've heard amazing things about it." She told me.

I took her hand. Made a solid serious eye contact. I held her right hand between my palms in a pleading manner.

"Meera, please?" I said in the same manner as the protagonist did in the movie's trailer.

It was some work but I ended up convincing her. We went to the theatre counter with the intention of buying a couple of tickets. She looked a bit worried.

"If you are not comfortable with the timing we can watch this movie later." I suggested.

"More alcohol." She exclaimed. Such a kid.

We decided to chuck the movie and go drink. (Why not?). When I say "We" I mean "Her". I didn't realise I was so consumed just being around her that everything she suggested sounded more fun than it would've been without her. We didn't drink much. She had 3 breezers and I had 3 pints of wheat beer.

I couldn't stop but wonder how I felt so good after such a long time. I had forgotten what happiness felt like. What I loved the most that night was we could share a comfortable silence for some parts. Or maybe I was imagining things. After the time in our bar we went out, sat on the side of the road and talked, waiting for our cab. If you've used Uber in India, you must know what a pain in the ass it is.

Uber drivers are very much like politicians in India, they promise things they can't deliver.

Be it a cab ride, the sight of true love or free wi-fi all over the city of New Delhi. False Prophets. But who really cares? They are not funded by my money. Meera on the other hand was all the reason I started loving late night's Uber rides. The more time we spend finding a cab, all the more time I get to spend with her. It wasn't love. It wasn't intense. It wasn't something I needed. It was something that made me happy which is better than most things.

Then there it was. The first defining moment of our story. There was a moment when we were just looking at each other and smiling. In that silent moment, all I could see was her hair blowing with the wind. All I could hear was the silent city traffic and swishing of high speed automobiles behind us. All the colour I could see was the Yellow signature Delhi street-lights shine on her face and the red of the traffic signal radiating through her hair. We were just looking at each other and smiling. I bet she didn't even notice but I bet my pupils dilated as much as they fucking could. Maybe like a puppy craving love. Puppies have a thing about them, they're cute. I am more like a hideous mixture of cute and arrogant. Just like Rahul Gandhi would be like on drugs. I mean how he would be naturally. He's on drugs all the time, isn't he? Who knows? Not me.

In my reluctant optimism, I believe there's a feeling in the back of someone's mind that they've always wanted. For some people, it is to have a certain car. For some people, it could be to make their parents proud. For me, it was that particular moment. There's a feeling in your head that you've pushed in a dark corner because it was never fulfilled. You pushed it back so hard that even you didn't know you want that feeling? You only know once that feeling comes to you. Destiny brings it to you. She was that feeling for me. She felt like happiness with a hint of redemption.

Then the cab came, we were going to her place first, so that I could drop her and go home. We shared our deep dark secrets as we moved towards out destination. And then there was a comfortable silence and eye contact. City lights have a way of making things more beautiful. The beauty felt endless and life seemed like a dream that came true.

"Abeer, don't get serious about me. Don't fall in love. Guys do and it makes everything a waste." She told me. Realisation hit. She was a rollercoaster, I was a fat kid, after eating to my fullest on a weak stomach.

Now I was in a dilemma. Either I could get all serious and lose an amazing friend or I could just play it cool. Playing it cool made more sense. She had a lot of emotional luggage. She didn't need more piled up by me. What I could rather do was help her get some of it off, if she'd let me. I couldn't blame the guys who went serious for her. Some people are meant to be admired, and some people are meant to be just friends. Life. It makes you look at what you've always wanted and how you can not have it. What was different this time she was not a thing, she was not a trophy. Having sex with her wouldn't make me happier about myself. Sticking around her would. Cultivating something bigger and better than what our natural reproductive instinct says. Obviously, I was confused about what I felt but I was sure of one thing. If she had said anything except what she said in the cab, I would've loved life a bit more. I could understand her perspective, she was to me the way I saw her. She knew I was falling for her and she couldn't let me do that. The fall usually breaks people. It didn't matter.

The only thing that mattered was why did I make myself vulnerable, again? Being a fuck-all dude is the easier way. Why be a lover when you can be a fighter? I was so tired of being someone I was not.

Life is the way easier when you don't have anyone to love. Life can be the way easier if the person you love is an asset and not a liability. Meera was both for me at the same time. I guess things could've been different if I was cool, mysterious and I have been that to woo girls.

There were a number of things I could say to look cool. I could lie. I could pretend but I didn't. I just sat there with confusion in my eyes and a smile on my face. She didn't know what she broke in me by saying that. I didn't know either. There was a storm coming. A storm that would blow me apart. There was a number of things you can say to woo a woman.

But this woman I didn't want to woo. This woman I wanted to love.

•••

The Side Effects of a Good Life

Everyone has something to look forward to in their lives. People all around. Have something they want to achieve and something they want to let go. Let me explain it to you. Some people around me craved fame and money. Some craved power and security. A few craved for drugs. A lot more craved for enough money to maintain a lifestyle that included a life full of super-cars and an endless supply of money. What did I crave? Obviously, I wanted to make a name for myself. I wanted not to live a regular life because of all the people I've met in my family's circle including some of Delhi's finest bureaucrats and millionaires. All I saw was unhappy children trying their best to find their identities, trying to outrun the huge shadows of their parent's success cast over them. These people were so busy living a life of glamour and power that they didn't value happiness. They only respected the people who matched their status or outdid them.

There were a few kids who just tried to exhaust their parents seemingly unlimited resources by acting out. They'd drink out of their minds and try to get trophy girlfriends just for the sake of killing time. Ambition was the last thing on their mind because they had everything on a platter. They had no real personalities or character strength to represent considering what their parents were. I pitied them. What kind of parent cares so little of their kid that they let them do whatever they wanted?

Some of the other kids worked very hard to make a career for themselves. They didn't want to be known as one of those kids who had their success handed to them by their parents. I was one of them. I wanted my parents to be recognised by my name. I spent most of my life back stepping and looking at the bigger picture. At one point, I'd realise the picture is endless and I stopped looking further. I just didn't know when to stop. Most of my life was spent trying to prove myself to my parents. I bet their lives had a similar pattern.

Very few of these kids were scared out of their mind. The dysfunction in their families had killed their spirits to live to such an extent that they were on the verge of mental breakdowns. Just a few years ago, one of the kids of my family friends gave up her life to depression. It is a losing battle, depression. The more you fight it, the deeper you go. Ignoring it is the best way to be a functional adult. That's what I thought them. Oh, what an ignorant asshole I was.

Whatever it was, I totally despised most people at these parties. There were only a few people who knew what the real world was all about. These kids lived their lives in such an extent of excess that they rarely had an opportunity to realise its value. I was one of them. Hence, the self loathing.

With all these different kids at these parties, one thing was common. They all craved for love and attention.

Coming back to the original question, what did I look forward to in life? I didn't want materialistic things. I didn't crave the money. I didn't crave power. I was happier sitting on a footpath with a stranger more than I was in an AC room. What did I crave? I wanted to make a name for myself but looking into the past I think that wasn't the answer either. It was just another materialistic need. Something made me feel that I was soon gonna know what I really craved.

"Everything seems like a mistake in retrospect." My father would always tell me.

Think about it, it is true. So, first thing to learn was to never look at things in retrospect. Who needs more mistakes on their shoulders? I knew I didn't. I never had any regrets. I probably won't. People only have regrets if they think about their past. I never took the time to do that. My life was only growing till that point of time. In this particular moment, it all felt like a mistake. Meera and I what not. It was difficult being in love and getting stomped on time after time. That's where I think I was wrong. Just maybe, looking at life in retrospect was the answer.

At this particular party, I had zero tolerance for bullshit. Why was this? Ever since I met Meera, I realised one thing. The world was not full of fuck-all kids with shallow ambitions and zero empathy. I was just always surrounded by them in these parties. It's funny when you look at the world from inside a bubble everything looks like wonderland. There was a particular kid in this group who'd always come to me to boast about some random girl he hit it and quit it with. It's just that, this time I wasn't taking his shit. So, I schooled the motherfucker and stepped out of the party. It's actually really easy to school shallow people. They won't learn either ways but I was taking every bit of satisfaction I got.

That's how I took her statement to the heart. Every time I closed my eyes, I'd see her face. Those eyes that turned cold faster than a teenager would come into his pants, thinking about Monica Belluci. That was the first time I felt like I didn't recognise her. Don't blame me, kid. I don't know how the human brain works, let alone the human heart. Maybe the reason was all the relationships I had in the past were less emotional. I loved out of loneliness and not out of love. I wasn't lonely anymore. I didn't want a relationship but it scared me how she just saw what was happening.

The second biggest lie of the universe is "No one can love you unless you love yourself first." The first lie being "God hates gays." I don't think in a world so fucked up, God's biggest concern is two gentlemen in love.

Everyone deserves love, maybe you can't love yourself because you expect too much out of you like I do. We are our biggest critics. We don't deserve love especially when we can't love ourselves. The important thing is to stay hydrated. Love finds a way. The luckiest are the people who come to love themselves because then they don't need anyone else. How beautiful is that? Being truly independent. So, this time why did I let myself be bothered by a statement made by someone I met a couple of months ago?

It wasn't who she was, it was what she said. Now the kind of damage a statement did to me, nothing else could. Even if my dad told me I was a disappointment I would've been like "Yeah, cool." I am someone you called a strong headed, deeply willed asshole. I never let people tell me who I was.

What could I do to find some comfort? How do you mend a situation like this? People would find a lot of ways to deal with this. Drugs were not an option, neither was alcohol because that's how people get addicted. I needed to figure out a permanent solution. What happened was that I would've been working my job (which was an amazing first job) and suddenly I would remember her face on that footpath with the lights and the sound. It would brighten up my chest and then send me in a zone of pure frustration. Angry not at her but at what a creature life is. But that's the demographic of helpless people, they love blaming life for their issues.

So I decided let me focus on life, my family, work and art. Art is always an escape. So I did what every sensible person on this planet would do. Whenever I had one drink too many, it sent me into a deep limbo of feeling nothing, not even enjoying the food I have always loved. I didn't want to kiss a stranger. The next morning, the hangover and taste of cigarettes in my mouth sent me off into a dilemma. Should I drink, smoke and enjoy life or Should I stop being a baby and man up? Now, all I could do was realise what I needed. What I liked and what I didn't. It was mostly things that brought us comfort were the most harmful for our progress. I wasn't letting my issues go to Meera because like I said before, she had enough emotional baggage. She didn't tell me about it but I knew it was there. It was as if I could see through her. We were two lonely people in a sea full of other people who made us feel more lonely. We don't want someone to talk to, we don't want someone to have sex with, we just need someone who we can be happy around. So, I decided to play it cool. Normal conversations. No neediness. No excessive flirting. No intense eye contact. Just whatever she likes, that's my top limit. Now, I am not a weak person who gets carried on by other people. I am usually the one with my hands on the wheel but for the first time, I chose to be the co-driver. She was mature, she knew what she was doing.

So, I manned up. I was gonna quit cigarettes, preferably stop excessive drinking. I would start spending more time with family and started to look for a therapists. I needed to know, why I went into this downward spiral by just one statement from someone I haven't known for a long time. The next morning, the hangover of someone else's actions. That made me feel weak. That's the last thing I want to be. As soon as I stepped out of the party, I put my earphones on, went looking for somewhere I'd wanna stop at.

I needed a break from all this. I needed a break from running away from things I needed and running towards things I wanted.

•••

The Therapist

Limbo. What do you think limbo feels like? How does it feel to be lost and forgotten? Somehow, Limbo always feels like a void to me. You know some of us have shut down their emotions to stop feeling hurt for a period of time and they end up feeling nothing. Why do you think teenagers often cut themselves with blades and pens? Why do you think an old man sits alone in a bar to have a few drinks? They just don't want to feel numb I think. That's how I felt now. I felt numb. What could I do about it? I guess, it was time to think and heal. If a dog bit you, and you ignored the wound it could very easily turn you rabid. If you get shots and deal with it, you'll probably maintain your stability. I decided I should go to a therapist and talk it out. I contacted a therapist recommended by a friend I met on Tinder. I would probably end up hooking up with this friend if I hadn't met Meera. Somehow, talking to her felt better than laying anyone else. Don't get me wrong, women are amazing. It's like God took their time to make them. That wasn't the main issue here. The main issue was that now all I saw in other people was their sadness and my whole focus went to trying to heal them. I didn't get attached to them. Attachment and assumptions are the downfall of the human race. Affection is the one thing that lifts them up. The capacity to love another more than you loved yourself. Mostly when you love someone more than yourself, you put them on a pedestal. That you don't see anything wrong in what they do. You build a justification in your mind for every incident that hurts you. It may seem like they shit gold, the sun shines out of their hair or God made them for you. Let me tell you something, God doesn't give a shit. God hates us all. Who gives a fuck anyway?

It was a usual Friday. I had walked out of work with a sad sigh. Why? I knew for the next couple of days I was gonna be free. That was the last thing I wanted to do. I didn't want to be free enough to think about Meera. I took a deep breath in.

"Gurgaon traffic smells like shit, doesn't it?" Shivangi asked.

It had been a long time since I had thought about her. Why was that? Elementary my dear reader, it was a thought worth suppressing. My chest hurt. Was I smoking too many cigarettes? I actually just had one cigarette that day. Was it anxiety? It was rare for me to have a panic attack when I was physically exhausted. I knew where I'd find some answers. I rushed to the therapist I had an appointment with.

It was a nice clinic near Sikanderpur metro station. What bothered me the most was that I was asked to pay for the session before I even saw the face of the therapist. Medicine has become a career rather than a vocation, hasn't it? Anyway, I ignored it as I had officially ran out of fucks to give. I just wanted to feel better. I went in, I shook her hand. She seemed like a decent person, but who doesn't look like a decent person anyway? So, I started talking. Without interruption. Without love. Without hatred. In a tone that was a cry out for help. What I laid out in front of the therapist was an abomination.

I didn't even realise all that I had left behind. I had come a long way, too bad it was the wrong way. It was like walking down a highway in congress era with utter bliss on my mind. Once you look back, all you see are potholes and broken street lights. There it was, the problem. Hidden in plain sight. A chain of broken hearts, crushed spirits, disregarded friendships, familiar hatred and unfamiliar love. Seldom do we realise what we are feeling till we talk to someone about it. Therapy is great.

I realised how everything was interconnected. How her telling me "Don't get serious for me, Abeer" hit me in a spot that was always very fragile. I don't like expressing my feelings, and she saw through everything. Her eyes always felt like it could pierce through everything, see what was meant to be seen. I loved how she looked at me. She knew what was going on in my head. Did I know what was going on in my head? Fuck no. In the history of time, someone saw through the charade. Trust me on folks, you have to choose in life. Don't love someone with your being if you want to be with them. You could never be with someone whom you loved more than yourself. I didn't love Meera more than myself. I loved her enough to think about what she needed, which was new for me. Finally, Not a man-baby eh.

I realised I was a dumb kid who was trying to figure things out and she was a grown woman who had heard everything I could tell her and seen every emotion to see that was coming her way. What I could offer her was happiness, a bit adventure and my company, which was not as bad it sounded.

What she could offer me was maturity, understanding and lips as appealing as whiskey on a Monday afternoon. Maybe the eyes that carried the promise to another heaven and late night hugs and cuddles that could make your heart stop. Haminastu. Look up that word. I was never a very sexual being but I crave the fuck out of some intimacy, if you know what I mean.

What do therapists actually do? Fuck if I knew. From what I had heard from the suicidal people I dealt on a regular basis it seemed like they just hear you without judgement or remarks. They just help you identify your own emotions so as to finally recognise yourself as a person. Isn't that what life is? The fight to find yourself while you inevitably change and evolve.

This particular therapist seemed mentally sound but then she colossally fucked up.

"When did the problem start?" She seemed confused.

"I have no fucking idea what the problem even is. I just don't wanna feel bad all the time. I don't wanna sit at parties and feel alone, you know?" I replied.

"I get that. What I am asking is what was the final trigger that made you come to me? Also, since when have you felt this way?" She replied.

"I've felt this way ever since I was shipped off to Kota. It felt like I lost a home. Now, even home doesn't feel like home. My family loves me but I feel like a guest." I replied.

"And what made you come here?" She was hitting the right spots looking blankly at me with a slight smile.

"Meera. Meera made me come here. I met her in an unexpected place and even though we are practically strangers something keeps pulling me towards her. I've never even paid attention to the hurt that has come my way from even close family but why do I suddenly care about what some random girl has to say? That's what made me come here." I was sure.

"What did she say?" The therapist was as curious.

I told her.

"Maybe Meera said what she said because she was scared. You know how someone wants to say something but they end up saying something else. Maybe all you need is patience. Maybe all you need is to focus on yourself while the world repairs itself around you." That was too much hope for a stubborn mind.

I didn't need promises. I didn't need guidance in love. I just needed someone to fix what was broken. It wasn't my bond with Meera, for all I knew or cared, mutual care was still a thing. Mutual love is probably rare and unexpected. But isn't everything worthwhile rare and unexpected? That's one of the issues I have with therapy and the self love culture. Every person who doesn't struggle with their pain and makes changes to their lives end up being a losers. That's how I was trained to see the world. Winners and losers. I didn't care if I was happy or not I just wanted to be a hell more successful. If I wanted eternal peace and acceptance I'd shave my head and become a monk.

So I heard everything the therapist had to say. All the bullshit she had to spew, all the promises she had to make. She was bullshitting a bullshitter. She was telling me what I wanted to hear and not what I needed to hear. I am a kid but I wasn't born yesterday. I left her office after the session got over, took a cab. In the back of the cab, while the driver was playing Bhojpuri songs it felt almost ironic how Bhojpuri songs are full of joy and how life wasn't so back then. Love hurts. I then remembered a story from the past. A story that needed addressing.

There was a friend of mine who loved a girl. The kind of love that comes once in a lifetime. The kid's love when he falls in love for the first time. Let's call the girl Devika and the dude Kartik. Kartik and Devika were my best friends from the first year of college. We were inseparable. We couldn't imagine our lives without each other. At least, I couldn't. Kartik fell in love with Devika from the moment he got to know her. Love at first site, if you will. Yours truly, on the other hand didn't see anything more than friendship around her. Sure, she was cute but who isn't if seen in the right perspective?

At one point of time, Kartik and Devika gave into the romantic tension and got into what you call a modern day relationship. For all the time their love blossomed I was home, chilling and drinking beer with random strangers. After a week of them dating, he rushed it and kissed her. The girl didn't like it. She broke it off with him and decided to be friends. Now, this was a classic scenario where Kartik thought Devika shit gold. To this day he believes it. Kartik didn't have any bad intentions and all he did wrong was rush into something, Devika wasn't comfortable with. Sure, it seems romantic in movies.

What we forget is, everyone is good looking here and there. If Hrithik Roshan kissed Katrina out of the blue, everyone would go "wow." If Shakti Kapoor did it, well he has done it already hasn't he. Where does the difference lie? Consent. It's a confusing fine line and I'd rather stay on the right side of it. The reason I am telling you all this is so that you learn from my mistakes. A year after their break-up Devika, Kartik and I had planned a trip to Kasol. Kartik had to pull out at the last moment but Devika and I, chose to go. It was then there that we zinged a bit. After almost six months of this trip, somehow, we ended up liking each other too. We were together for two months. That relationship was an adventure and I don't regret it.

I just regret everything that happened when it ended. Seeing how Kartik felt for that girl, it was obvious that he was heartbroken. I can't even imagine the pain of seeing the guy you've been best friends for two years be in "love" with a girl you've loved for two years.

Devika on the other hand likes being a victim and Kartik was more than happy to be a shoulder to cry on. In all this while, a girl had a shoulder to cry on, a guy had his crush's attention again and I had no one. Somehow, I had seen people around me trying to play victims in any fucking given scenario. I had seen women and men seeking sympathy for even cheating on their partners. I bet you've too. It's just easy to blame the other person and not hold yourself accountable for your actions isn't it?

Just because I dated the girl, doesn't mean I was the winner in this scenario. People would tell you that dating someone is "kick-ass" or an achievement. Relationships are work and my dear friends, my experience says nourish your relationships. Don't be with anyone who hurts you, no matter how much you love them. You will be a ghost in a dark room smoking a cigarette listening to Pink Floyd. Since, I never made any other friends in college I was practically alone all this while. That hurt like a bitch. Before I knew it, I was sleeping for straight fifteen hours, missing classes, falling sick and having a series of anxiety attacks. There was a time I didn't leave my hostel room for four days and no one had noticed. I would've been dead and no one in Patiala would know. That experience taught me the art of living alone and pulling yourself out of a shit storm. What it taught Kartik was the fact that it's not necessary you end up with someone just because you love them. What it taught me was that Devika was toxic for both of us and I had to pull out. He wasn't going to. No matter how much you love someone, how much you miss them there is a time when you rise above them and move on. I did that. I am telling you this story maybe because that's why I wasn't that disappointed when I wasn't ending up with Meera like I ideally should've. We had understanding, mutual respect, our fair share of happiness but love isn't about that. Love is about being with someone who doesn't give a shit about you. I cared about Devika but I never paid much attention to her. I never gave her the time of my life. Kartik on the other hand hated how much she was drawn to me even when he was doing all he could for her. He would talk to her for hours, he would love her and care about her.

What was the result of this whole scenario? Devika dated me over him. Why? It's human tendency not to want something that is readily available for you. Everything we get for free seems like a scam. It is very easy to fall for someone who cares about you but doesn't love you. Loving someone who already loves you is like playing a video game easily. No one wants to do that.

People want adventure. People want an impossible love to bloom and wield unexpected blissful circumstances. Meera was my muse. Honestly, she could be my favourite person on planet earth right next to Bella. In this pursuit, nothing else mattered but what it felt like just to be around her and how she felt around me. Meera, had the same battle. She was a Kartik for someone else. She loved someone dearly. She gave her everything to him. I bet at some point of time, she would do anything to keep him around. People are desperate like that. They want to be loved. They don't want to be loved just by anyone, they want to be loved by someone special, and not getting this love could kill their chance at romantic happiness. In her story, her boyfriend was what I was to Devika. Maybe I cared for Devika, Maybe I thought she was pretty but I never cared enough if you take into account how much Kartik cared. Every person has been a Kartik, a Devika and an Abeer at some point of their lives. Every Devika would know the love of a Kartik but would still date an Abeer. They will see the Kartik's sacrifices as trivial while they would see even a menial deed done by an Abeer as a blessing. They would justify everything an Abeer did because love teaches a person how to forgive.

Every Kartik would have to move on and know that you cannot love someone you have put on pedestal. You can pray to a Goddess, you can't play with her and kiss her like it was the end of the world.

Every Abeer would need to realise that love isn't a game and there is nothing worse in this life than to hurt someone who counted on you. Every Abeer would realise that maybe it was time to be true to himself.

Truth be told, Kartik and Devika were in a way better place now than I was. They had goals. They saw a future. I was just living life on Autopilot. I never wanted something bigger for myself except to feel like home somewhere. Somewhere, someone looks at me with eternal love for whom I was enough, not my potential. What a kid.

What's funny is that all of us pass judgements on our friends in their romantic experiences but we don't even follow our own advice when we end up in one. My heart just said Meera was someone this asshole could appreciate after developing the habit of living alone. I didn't want to be a Kartik, a Devika or an Abeer. I just wanted to be better than all of those for her. She deserved a lot of love. All of them were kids who didn't know what to do with love. What to do with their lives. A lot of them still don't know. Maybe it was time to forgive myself and learn. You can do it, Kid. It's okay to be a fool in love. Just don't give up every happiness for the promise of lost love, don't love someone more than your being and don't be confused what you want like Devika.

The taxi ride ended, I entered Delhi metro. Somehow, I exited at Jor Bagh metro station. It was because I saw this girl standing on the metro station. A girl who used to be my best friend. Jahnavi. She was a Kartik in love. I stopped talking to her because how she would justify everything her ex would do to her. She welcomed me with the same smile and a warm hug.

"Abeer, are you okay?" She asked me.

Jahnavi was a kind girl. She was of the same height as me. She had short hair now. She was reading a book at a metro station.

Her hands were still bigger than mine and now she was clearly over the superficial things she was into a couple of years ago.

I was about to probably shed a well timed tear but I held it back. Time was still. Kudos to human kindness. After all this while, she saw through the charade. It was then that I realised, love is eternal and not limited to a place or person.

It stays if it has to. Remember that. I talked to her, we walked in the colony just like the old days. While saying goodbye, I gave her a kiss on the forehead and told her I was sorry. That I was too dumb to understand what she was going through and that now I will be here for her if she wants me to be. Something told me she had moved on from the friendship, so did I. Funny how things work themselves out temporarily. We just looked at each other and smiled with kindness. Forgiving each other for being dumb kids. Loving each other for the amazing memories we had.

•••

He knew, She Obviously Knew

Delhi Metro. Another thing I loved about Delhi. It was not that it had a good mode transportation, it was the kind of people I saw throughout the journey. Happy people, sad people, stressed people and most importantly the late night drunk ones. While working in Gurgaon and living in East Delhi, a huge part of my free time went into commuting but it was kinda fun. Why? Let me explain it with an example, I was waiting for a metro at Sector 54 Rapid Metro station in Gurgaon on a fine evening. Every person once in their life should see a winter sunset from any metro station in Gurgaon. You'll notice the sky turns pinkish and that light reflects from the floor of the platform and if you have the strength to walk to one end of the platform to look at the short Gurgaon skyline you'll notice that every place is beautiful. Just at different points of time. Just like people.

On that particular evening, there was a guy who was standing by me looking at the sunset. We looked at each other and smiled, then we continued looking back at the skyline. I had no mental space to talk to someone on that day, so I just started putting my earphones on. When I just plugged the right one in, his phone rang. His ringtone was "Shine on you crazy diamond" by Pink Floyd and I saw the name of the caller on his phone; "Mrs. Always Right".

I couldn't help but laugh. It's cute isn't it? This guy was at least six feet tall and he was muscular as hell. You know the kind of men who'd win a fist fight against a bear? Like an Indian take on Thor, I'd say. His forearms and neck were covered with tattoos that done were in good taste.

"I am so sorry, baby. I'll be right there. Don't kill me please. I'll get you burgers." He was explaining being late maybe. I could hear her shouting on the other end.

"I'll get you extra fries…" He smiled at me.

"Just come home." I could hear her say that on the other end of the phone.

He cut the phone and let out a sigh.

"What happened?" I was curious.

"I promised her I'll be home early today but my manager loves me too much." He laughed.

"Does that actually work? Getting food to solve any argument?" I didn't know what to ask.

"Dude, there is no relationship problem food, good sex or vodka can't solve." He seemed sure.

"Oh yeah… Heard that before." I was drained of any energy to get humour.

"You seem like a mess. Relationship issues?" He asked me.

"Not really… Maybe… I don't know." I was unsure.

"You've been playing with your lighter for the past ten minutes without even knowing…" He told me.

"You could say I had a hectic day at my office." I didn't want to share much about my personal life because it's difficult explaining it.

The train was there. He boarded it. I wanted to appreciate the sunset for the time it lasted before I headed on home. There I sat on the platform looking out at the glory of the Gurgaon and the corporate jungle it had become. I don't mean it in a bad way. There was a particular building I loved out of all of them, I don't have any idea what building it was. You know there are somethings in life that you want to observe from a distance, you don't want to know more about it. You just want to feel it.

The next day, I had to board a train to Aligarh. Why can't work trips ever take you to places like Srinagar or Goa? Fuck it. It's actually hard to be struggling with depression while working a job, having a family, loving a confused beautiful woman and having other ambitions in the field of art. Let's just say, I was working hard enough to replace depression with exhaustion. There was no one I could share my condition with. My best friend had disappointed me over and over again. Meera had her own stuff to deal with. Everyday, I would wonder if I could tell my family. I already knew the answer to it.

Whatever you do kid, never let anyone in your family know you're depressed. It's a brown people thing. One sick member sends the whole regime in an unending panic. It is a vicious circle. If your parents know you're sad/depressed, they either shower you with questions about it or they panic and go paranoid, either ways it only makes things worse. You know how people sometimes being sweet and amazing try to help you but instead just push you down the drain more. Don't get me wrong, I am thankful to my family. They are amazing, they are patient, they've loved me regardless of my never-ending self loathing. So was with my friends, we were all pillars to each other. We never hurt each other anymore, that function was in the jurisdiction of the rest of the world. We just met, smoked up, played football, pet our common dog and roast each other. My office, my seniors and coworkers are all amazing people. They work hard, they party harder and they are really caring. Showing weakness either physical or mental at work is the worst mistake you can ever make. You are not there to socialise, you are not there to make lifelong friends. I already have them. You are at work to work, have fun, chill around a bit and miss home or a loved one. Either ways whenever a coworker of mine discussed his love life, it ended with everyone competing on how many Tinder matches everyone had. Trivial things. But the age old question remains.

Why am I telling you all this? It was because it was impossible to show any negative emotion in front of anyone around me. Why? They wouldn't understand. They would try to but fail. Every time I had shown weakness in my life, I had lost a few people. I bet most of you have seen that.

I tried telling a friend and he spent the rest of the evening trying to convince me that it was just infatuation. I gave him the benefit of doubt but I couldn't consult with him further because he would not understand how deep this problem lied in my head.

It wasn't about a person. It was about a feeling. People can easily forget you but they'll never forget how you made them feel. That is exactly why I needed to talk to her. She made me happy. No one else had that capacity anymore. I have no idea why.

Most of our conversations were late night. Why? She couldn't sleep and I didn't want to. Night time was always valuable to me. It's when you feel the most, also when you as an artist can create the most. Besides the, city lights that I could see from my room's window were always my muse. I would utilise this time to paint, sketch or read. My favourite activity for this time now was talking to Meera. Whatever else I did, I would go to sleep with a void in my chest but when I went to sleep after talking to her, it would feel pretty fucking great. Peaceful, too. Weird how love works. There is a thing about love, it is one of the most rewarding and beautiful feelings out there but it comes at the risk of your own happiness. The issue being reciprocation. Not getting the love from someone you love wholeheartedly is a greater health hazard than sitting on a radioactive piece of uranium. The issue being uranium will probably give you ass cancer but one sided affection mostly takes all the beauty away from the world. All this while, there was a tune I found, that made me think of her somehow and I played it repeatedly, until I would fell asleep. Do I wanna know? If this feeling flows both ways. Kinda hoping that she'd stay. Baby, we both know that the nights were only made for saying things you can't say tomorrow day. (Hell yes, I quoted one my favourite songs. Even Elton John loves it.)

So I was in a city called Aligarh. I had a feeling it wouldn't be called so in a few months. (Remember what happened to Allahabad?) I was visiting a client, all the work was going great and I was keeping myself busy. Keeping yourself busy is the oldest trick in the book to get your mind-fucked. Ignoring issues only increases them. That's why people working in corporations have frequent mental breakdowns or mid-life crises. At the end of the day I was coming back to my hotel, the cab driver dropped me near the railway station which was around 2 kms away from my hotel. I loved walking in the evening. So, I started walking and opened up google maps to get directions. What I see next is there was a theatre by her name around 300 metres from my Hotel. Wow, exactly what I needed. So with all these thoughts blowing up my mind, I decided it's time to send her the notes that I hadn't shown her. I didn't know a better way to say anything because looking at her, it felt that to her love was just a word now. She had seen everything, heard everything and loved someone with her whole heart and she saw them go. When one word is repeated over and over again in life, when it is misused and mistreated, the word loses it's meaning. I didn't want to tell her I think I love her because that's the last thing anyone wanted to hear.

I didn't know much but my instincts worked pretty well around her. Somehow, I always knew what she needed and maybe that's why it felt so good.

After reading the notes the only thing she replied with was a grammatical error I made in a whole field of things I wrote. I wasn't surprised. Who wants to talk about something they don't want? Kids, something you need to realise. Unwanted love can also be as hard to people as unrequited love is. So she called me, it was around two am I guess. We both worked our asses the whole day, we needed rest. We didn't want it somehow. There was a show I used to watch, How I met your mother. While the whole show was mostly casual fun, there was one line that I couldn't shake off. The protagonist Ted Mosby used to say, "Kids, when it is two am go to sleep. Nothing good ever happens after two am"

That time, Meera seemed vulnerable and exhausted. That wasn't who she was, she would probably beat up a thousand engineering employees at her flight before showing vulnerability.

There was a certain sadness in her voice, something heartbreaking was coming my way. My dear reader, always kick into your instincts when it comes to love.

Naturally, I asked her, "What's wrong Meera?"

"I don't.. I don't know….. You know ever since I have been an adult I always knew my parents weren't around, but now out of all the times, I miss them so much."

That broke my heart a bit. Not what she said, the way she said it. The feeling in her voice that at the same time was breaking apart and keeping itself together. The fact that if she didn't miss them then and she misses them now, it must be because she is hurt more than she ever was. You know how a kid always runs to a parent when they're hurt, no matter where they are. Even you, in the moments of your immense pain, must've called your mother once right?

I somehow knew something else was coming my way. So, I just tried to hear because this is the first time she was trying to talk. I stayed silent because I didn't know what I could say to make anything better. How do I do anything here? How do I say something worth saying. I realised I didn't have anything to contribute, to console or to eradicate the pain and so I kept mum.

The same day I confronted her so as to what was fucking up. Confrontations have a thing about them, they are absolute. They don't leave a scope for resolution if they turn ugly. I was ready. Either it would be a creep or a concerned person in her life. I guess I wanted to know what did she consider me of these options. I have a habit of developing pain where there shouldn't be any. Habits are weird too. Either they are good or they are bad. Some people are habitual smokers, some have a habit of waking up early and being productive. I have a habit of fucking up everything I care about. Maybe because I am scared of love, maybe because I don't have the balls to follow through. But all I could think of all these days when I thought about Meera was when we were sitting outside Lord of the Drinks waiting for a cab. How happy we were. I knew for a fact that I wasn't that happy when she wasn't around. Maybe that's where it went wrong. Maybe that's where it felt right.

So what I did was absolutely any idiot would do, I wrote up the draft and I emailed it to her. She always knew I had a thing for her, I knew that too. But I never told her anything from my perspective. So I did. She read the whole thing and guess what was her first response.

"Abeer, everything you say I've heard before. That's what happens, either my friends fall for me or they get away and I am left alone." Now I have known for a fact what loneliness is, it's not that you don't have anyone around you.

Loneliness is when there are a lot of people around you and yet no one sees or understands you. In that moment I made a decision. Helping her be happy was more important than these hormones.

Naturally being a dumbfuck retard ass bonafide stupid fuck I initiated a series of statements.

"You say every guy who is your friend starts liking you, how do you choose who you want to be with?"

"See, the last guy, he just made me feel amazing. It felt like there was this feeling of unreal happiness around him.

Like there is this feeling in the back of the head that you've always wanted. And I got that feeling with him. It was like I was alive."

And then it hit me. That's a fucked up feeling. What it can do to people.

It's just life. Like love, life has way to fuck you up too. That's why kids, love yourself. Other people always disappoint. If someone could disappoint Meera, I was just an average creature.

•••

Is This Depression? Fuck If I Know

"Why do you come home late these days?" asked my Mother. "I have to commute from Gurgaon. It's an hour and a half away. I am new at the company so I have to put more work in." I told her.

Somehow, she never believed it. I have no idea why. This was not the first time I was being questioned about my whereabouts. I can't blame her, I was always very casual about my career. If you look at my face, you'd notice that it is the face of someone who doesn't know what he's doing in life and still manages to do pretty well.

The next day Meera had her third round of screening and I was sure that she would get in. She didn't. I was concerned that she would've been a bit sad at least. Like I told you, she would never show vulnerability when it wasn't out of her very capable hands. So, we talked in the evening I told her to tell me if she wants to have dinner. She said sure she would. I had a thing that night that I totally forgot about. I had to go to a ramleela with my family. A close family friend organised the whole deal near the Red Fort. It was around 10 pm. I saw that there was a missed call from her so I called her up.

She asked with a certain freshness in her voice, "Weren't we gonna have dinner together?"

"Sure tell me where you wanna go?"

"You tell me"

"Lord of the drinks, CP?"

"Sure."

I told my family that Siddharth needed to see me and that I had to rush. So I did.

I reached lord of the drinks, she was wearing the same dress from when we were last there. Everything was exactly the same except the familiarity we carried.

"My treat." She implied.

I just agreed. I was running low on funds too and I didn't have the energy to say anything after this long torn day spent in an ankle cast.

We decided on shots. Shots are the way to be. There is nothing in this world that Vodka can't fix.

I needed a drink too. I had a feeling she did too.

We didn't talk much that night. All she did was look at the people dancing, having fun on the dance floor. All I did was look at how happy she was doing that. I didn't smoke that night.

She didn't have a thing against it but it just didn't feel right. Also, I only smoke with company or under extreme exhaustion. At one point, there was a song that came on. A song she loved. She took my hand forgetting about my ankle injury took me to the dance floor. And then we danced. I couldn't do much. Still the time I had was pretty good. I saw her dancing, having fun, being a dork and that weird genuine smile on her face.

At one point she just stopped, came to me and said, "You'll fall in love.". I didn't realise I wasn't dancing anymore, I just stood there looking at her and smiling. She wasn't wrong. What is love even if not wanting to see someone each day without feeling a hint of boredom.

"You've got nice moves." I suggested.

She looked at me, sort of offended and just walked off.

I didn't know what was on her mind. I asked her, "What happened?"

"What did you say on the dance floor?!"

"You've got nice moves. What's wrong with that?"

"Oh."

Then I realised it. In that chaos of dance floor she actually heard something else entirely.

Damn, such a kid.

Then we went back to the dance floor after a while. Danced it out. I had a conversation with her best friend on how it was my responsibility to get Meera home safely. It was a sweet gesture.

Why am I telling you all this? So that you can know what kind of situations shaped my thought about Meera. On our way back in the cab, we were talking, joking and we argued a bit about Aam Aadmi Party. She had volunteered for it. I am from a family of bureaucrats. See how we are at odds? Could've been a Shakespearean story if we actually fell in love. That's one of the things I love about her. She actually works for what she believes in. She doesn't sit and pass judgements. I, on the other hand, am a lazy ass artist. I don't work, I don't volunteer. I just want to create and express. So I looked at her, as lovingly as I always did. She realised I didn't want to fight about something so trivial. She agreed. She was the smarter one obviously. She asked me if I had backups, as in someone to fall back to. I didn't have an answer to that. I never thought of it that way. I never needed someone to fall back to. God-forbid this turns out as it is destined to, I will just fall back into the subtle art of loneliness. Which is not a bad thing necessarily, it gives me space to create. So I told her, "I don't think I need backups." She looked the other way and said, "Every guy lies anyways."

Somehow, it wasn't what she said that I thought about. It was what she felt. Loss and pain. I told her, "Let the guys be. Focus on your happiness right now." I didn't know what to do or say. I just took her hand, kissed it and held it. She placed her head on my shoulder. My urban short lived romance. City lights passing by us, 70's Bollywood music in the background and Meera's hand in mine. I said what I never should've, "Meera, I didn't think it was possible for me to feel this good." She didn't say anything. She stayed there. It could've been a minute or an hour I wouldn't know. Time has a thing about it. Sometimes you lose the concept of it. So when she felt better she faced me and we talked and laughed as usual. Nothing was odd. Nothing felt special. Everything that was happening felt natural. We reached her place, I met her sister. We talked, laughed and teased Meera a bit. Then she ordered a cab for me. Went downstairs to drop me off.

Before I entered the cab she hugged me. You know, you can never know how much you craved affection until someone hugs you harder than usual and you never want to let them go. I had to. I could've stayed there for the rest of my lonely life. I probably could've kissed her.

I could've done a thousand things at that point of time but what I chose to do was give her a peck on the cheeks and go home. I didn't want to do anything that she didn't want. Honestly, it didn't cross my mind then. My head was as clear as the air in New Delhi. If you've been to Delhi you have a good idea of what I am talking about.

•••

Damini. Also, The Ugly

"I think you've healed a lot. You've worked a lot on yourself and I see amazing results. I think we should start meeting once in two weeks and see how you react to it." Said Damini, my second therapist.

I had many sessions with her which I don't think would be fruitful to write about. It was just about a confused mind, babbling. Pouring it's heart out. I've started to believe in the pursuit of having everyone's back. Treating everyone with the respect and care they seldom deserve, I didn't have anyone to shit my feelings on. My feelings which still seem so unimportant, that I keep them bottled up. I don't know why they have always been my lowest priority in life. Somehow, I get the feeling I could never fix that on my own. So, I did what any sensible adult should do. All of this seemed to be coming to an end. I was more social, I ate healthier, I slept better, I drank a lot of water and I smoked a lot lesser. The smoking part didn't feel so good. Cigarettes are my answer to sadness, stress or love. It almost felt better. Everything felt like it was going to be alright. "Yeah, I do still have some issues to deal with. I think I can deal with them one step at a time". It was a relief because at one point of time Damini suggested that I needed anti-depressant. She subtly suggested it because she knew my thought process that was very much in need of medication. I refused and tried to work myself through everything. It felt like a victory, getting out of therapy.

Stepping out of that office, I took a deep breath and observed how beautiful an evening it was. Kailash colony, New Delhi. Everything seemed beautiful. I plugged in my earphones, it was almost winter. Winter is the best season for me. You can walk more without the stress of sweating, you can wear jackets and sweatshirts but most importantly winters seem like the only season in which the world is beautiful. I could never appreciate a bright summer morning but give me a cold dark night and I would fall in love. I started walking, I didn't know where I was going. I walked past happy smiling strangers and after a while I realised I was smiling too. There was no reason to it. It wasn't because I read something funny. It wasn't because of my dark sense of humour. I didn't remember the last time I smiled without a reason. Walking past everything I could feel the need to talk to someone or meet someone. It was a Saturday. Most people were free but who did I want to see? Obviously, Meera was a strong contender but I thought at this point of time I want to see Siddharth more. I thought he would appreciate how happy I was, he had been really concerned about me. Both of us were sad and beaten up, yet both of us always put the other person first. Maybe, that's what friendship is. Maybe that's why my standards in friends went so up. So I drank a whole bottle of water in one go and took an auto to Siddharth's. I loved how beautiful everything seemed. How beautiful the world actually was.

From a kid running with tyre on the footpath, to my Auto driver listening to "Tamanche pey disco" everything seemed like it was on it's prime. The warm feeling in my chest was back about Meera. With no regrets, this time. No guilt.

Once I reached Siddharth, I met Bella. Our dog. She was going to be an year old soon. Every time she saw me she would pee herself in excitement. Bella is one of the brightest things in my life. Isn't that what dogs are supposed to be? A beacon of light for people to remind themselves that someone can love them unconditionally? I went and sat down with Siddharth. I told him about the chain of events, it was almost poetic the way his face changed after he heard the news. He was rolling a joint and I was ready to smoke up. Now, you should know, drugs are pretty great if you don't get addicted. Remember that. We smoked up, talked and laughed. I told him how my life was going, he told me how his life had been. I updated him on where I think I was with my job, with my family and Meera. He updated me on how his family was, how Bella misses me and how his ex continues "hoe-ing around". We just lied down, picked up right where we left it off. On my way to the therapist, I got a call from Meera. She told me she was back in Delhi, my first thought was that I wanted to spend Saturday night with her. But it wasn't happening one way or another. There were a lot of things I knew about Meera and a lot of things that I can't comprehend. I was gonna know that by 4 am the next morning. I told Siddharth how I wanted to take Meera to Pianoman Jazz Club tonight and he just got up and said, "Dude, we should do something. I totally forgot it was a Saturday." Now there was this girl Siddharth and I knew for sometime. Siddharth matched her on tinder and they were good friends. I don't get why people make friends on tinder. So, we called her up and asked her if she wants to do something.

"Yeah sure, I am free. What do you want to do?"

"Let's watch a movie. You, me and Siddharth."

"Sure, sure. Come to my place we can smoke up and watch a movie here."

I forgot she had her own apartment. So we went to Gurgaon, where her apartment was. I entered the room and saw how beautifully she had decorated everything, how she had polaroids on the wall of her friends she missed how there were bookmarks in the middle of books she wasn't reading anymore. She was a great host. We watched a movie and I was just digging through her books. We bonded over how we love Gurgaon's corporate jungle. How this is the hub for ambition in North India. It was nearly 2 am when we were talking about dumb things and I received a message from Meera. It said, " Something happened here." I knew that she was gonna see her cousin Jasleen, and probably drink up a bit. So I didn't know what kind of thing she was talking about. What could possibly happen to two girl drinking some booze in the confines of their comfortable home.

"What happened?"

"We went to the club and there was a fight."

My face changed, there was an instance in which there was

a mixture of pure fury and worry on my face if I think about it. I went into the room, where Siddharth and Sakshi were. I told Siddharth, "It's time to go." Siddharth noticed my face and he just said, "Thank you Sakshi. You were a great host but it's kinda late and we gotta go home." When we went out he asked me, "What Happened with Meera?"

I didn't even tell him anything but he always knew what was going on my mind and what I needed. So, we started driving to Delhi. I had asked Meera to call me if or when she gets a chance. She did, she told me what happened.

Friends of Meera's cousin got into a fight with Bouncers and got beaten up pretty bad. I still don't know how to feel about situation but it isn't my place to feel or pass judgements. It was about her. All I cared about if she was okay. So Siddharth drove as fast as he could, I told her that we were coming. We got them a few shirts or sweatshirts because that was the only thing she asked for. I imagined a classic hospital scene with her sitting outside on a bench with her friends. When we reached the Hospital, it was a white Jaguar they were sitting in. Their laughter audible outside the vehicle. I knocked on the door, gave her the bag which had the clothes and stood outside with Siddharth. Siddharth and I already knew what happened. We had seen enough clubs and rich Delhi dudes to know. I still didn't want to pass judgements and hoped they were better than the people I knew. Something gave me the feeling it wasn't so. Since, the dawn of time the only thing that's constant is how women love them bad rich dudes. All I had on my mind was how this guy instead of dropping these girls off, had them sit in a car parking lot at 3:30 a.m. Siddharth, Meera and I talked for a bit after she stepped out. She seemed fine, I on the other hand didn't know what to do or say. Siddharth and Meera, talked and I couldn't think of words I wanted to say. I don't know what was on my mind. I was relieved she was fine and happy with her friends. I don't know why I was sad, almost disappointed. I didn't know what I was disappointed in. Meera or I. When I think about Meera, there was nothing wrong about the situation and it was almost her usual mature self that knew how to deal with it. When I think about me, I was so worried. And to think that she didn't see what was going on there. I did. I didn't have the full picture and I still don't. I have been in enough ugly situations to know how they turn out. Siddharth and I both had an idea of what may have happened and if you've roamed the streets of Delhi enough, you do too. All my sense, all my carelessness went down the drain when it came to her. It was killing me. I didn't have anything to say, anything to do. So I did what I could, I told her, "You should probably go to your friends, they need you more than we do. Siddharth and I will just smoke a joint and chill." Siddharth and I both knew we weren't going to chill. Both of us knew it wouldn't be so. The only thing I've ever lied to Meera about is my issues. As I've told you my dear reader, there was no scenario in this where Meera gets my emotional baggage. I should've been fine if she was. But I wasn't. I went outside, and I smoked a cigarette. I told you at the beginning of this chapter. Cigarettes are my answer to sadness, stress or love. It was all three at the same time.

We went back to the car. Siddharth suggested that we should ask Meera if she needed to be dropped off. I knew for a fact she wouldn't leave her friends behind. Integrity is her thing. Maybe that's why I loved her. Love is weird in the wrong places. This is the first time I am telling you that I for a fact thought I loved her because now when I think about it, in that parking lot I just wanted to hug her and let out a sigh of relief. Something told me she didn't want it and neither did I at that point. So, after much pressure from Siddharth, I asked her.

I told Siddharth while typing out the message, "Dude, she is comfortable with her friends. Let her be. She needs to be with them. She chose to be with them. We insisted to be here, she didn't ask us to. It was just that I wanted to see if she was really okay. She is. You saw that she seems comfortable, right?"

She didn't need us to drop her.

She told me "We have our car at CP. We'll go there." I already knew, it was all good and done. She was fine. "We are leaving the hospital now, you should too." By the time we were leaving, the Jaguar was already gone. It was happening all over again. Life in black and white. When Siddharth and I made plans to visit Sakshi, it was because we agreed that we need to do something exciting tonight. Get off our asses. Like the old times. Siddharth and I drove back to his place, I checked the time. 4:00 a.m., my usual time to sleep. I didn't feel sleepy at all, I didn't need love. All I needed was reassurance that something this dumb won't happen again. Rich dudes getting in fight with bouncers is a bigger cliché than a boy falling for a girl, a girl that doesn't want him. Driving in a cold winter night, what used to be my favourite thing to do. Delhi street lights passing by us when we weren't talking, just listening to the violent winds passing us by. The same winds that seemed so friendly 4 hours ago. We reached his place, Bella welcomed us in her usual fashion. She peed herself in excitement. I don't know if anyone else was as excited to see me as Bella always was. I petted her. We took her to the terrace, there were two beds up there. Siddharth lied down in one and instantly slept. I on the other hand watched the sunrise with Bella's head in my lap. Whenever I was at Siddharth's place, Bella would sleep in the bed I slept in. The cold winter night had passed, for the first time in my life I appreciated the sun. Even though, it brought skin cancer, sweat and heat it also shed some light. Light of clarity. I just finished another cigarette, hugged Bella and went to sleep.

•••

Aren't Birthdays Amazing?

"Why are heartbreaks so common?" asked Shivangi. Was this another nightmare? I wouldn't know. Nightmares were clearly the most regular thing in my life at this point of my life. Life was like a nightmare, too. I had no idea what I was doing with my life, but then again who the fuck did? There are usually two kinds of dreams I've encountered. The first ones are so good that you regret waking up and the second ones are dark enough that they spoil the next day. Either way, everything is a nightmare. Except Meera.

I had made a pact with myself that I will share everything I write, with Meera. So, that I don't get anything wrong. So that Meera wasn't judged by me. Also, very importantly I loved writing for her. I never had written more than just a word I shared with her what I was going to write about the night at the hospital knowing well how it could be misinterpreted in the extreme and how it could as well get our much awaited trip to Shillong cancelled. I was willing to take that chance. Sure, life would've been hard. I made a few promises to myself, everything else is flexible, really. This rule wasn't. The next day, I woke up feeling like shit. I checked the time, it was 8:30 a.m. I had slept for 3 hours at best. It was time to go home. Siddharth was sleeping so I didn't think to disturb him. I fed Bella, said a short and sweet goodbye and left for home. The nearest metro station was 6 kms. I had time. So, I started walking. I walked to metro station. Blank. I didn't know if I overthought the whole situation last night. Unapologetically so. I would never apologise for what got Meera in the situation but I could apologise to Meera if she got the wrong idea. Why? Because

I am many things, I am a bit opinionated but Meera wouldn't change in my eyes by something so trivial. It was easy to believe I was judging her, but I wasn't. I was judging the situation to my best of capacity. I called the last chapter the Ugly not because the situation was Ugly. It was more about how everything turned so ugly even at the thought of her being a bit hurt. I was glad she was okay, I was glad she was laughing with her friends in a car. I was just tired. Deep in thoughts, I reached the metro station. My phone had been dead since we left for Siddharth's place from the hospital last night. Back in the metro, there was a man trying to woo his girl. In all this while, he was being pretentious and talking to her while she was looking somewhere else. No expressions on her face. No sense of interest. I was just calmly observing the situation and what it turned out to be was the guy was another Kartik. I missed the dude. I made a list of things to do, on the unforgiving Sunday.

1. Write a short story.
2. Call Kartik and Devika.
3. Lie in your bed till you feel better.

When I reached home, my mom stood there with utter indifference.

My Mother was an amazing woman but I had tested her in manners incomprehensible to someone who had a life like mine. She tried to keep everything together, while everything had been falling apart since the dawn of time. My parent's story is not mine to tell. All I can say is they did their best in a toxic situation, raise me and my brother up in abundance of things. We didn't live in a world of needs but a world of wants. So, it was only logical that she was a bit disappointed when all I did was work, party, sleep and be distant. I could see that all she wanted was my time and I would gladly hand it to her.

Somehow, the distance between us over the past few months had only grown. So I added another element to the list:

4. Talk to Ma.

Then I just spent the day around her while she texted, scrolled through Instagram or watched Crime Patrol sort of shows. I texted Meera a bit. She realised something was off. "You don't sound like yourself." said Meera. What could I tell her that could make her feel better? So I called her and talked for a bit. Then I sat down and wrote "The Ugly." Why? It was an important part of how my psyche revolved around her. Not everything can be perfect in a story right? It was a dark night but nothing had changed in my mind one bit for Meera. Given the same circumstances I would take the same steps without doubt but this time instead of being just worried, I would be worried and funny. That's what's necessary in situations like these. That's what she knew. That's where there is a thin line of maturity. I sent her that email. I bet she read that. As soon as possible then came a time of not texting, not responding to calls. "Let's talk when she wants to." I told myself. So it was evening now. I got up took a shower. I realised I had spent a whole day in bed. Again. I decided to go out, even when I didn't want to. It was Siddharth's birthday eve. No matter my mood, he deserved better. So we friends hung out, chilled out and drank a bit. We celebrated his birthday like it should be celebrated. Even Bella was as excited as she had ever been. After everyone left, Siddharth and I sat down. We talked how we met when were fifteen. Now we were both twenty two. Looking at the time, it just felt like it was a very different world. We decided to do something that we used to do back when were kids. We went for a drive. Meera was still very pissed with me but that was our problem. Siddharth realised there was something but we didn't talk about it. Why? It was his birthday. I didn't want it to be a bad one. Siddharth and I, we didn't even have a sip of whiskey. We were the people who took care of every dude that was passed out or the ones who seemed chaotic. Most drunk Delhi guys were either Joker from The Dark Knight or Tom from 500 days of summer. They either wanted to see the world burn or they wanted to bitch about a girl who didn't have the capacity to love them. So went on a sober drive, just like we did when we were eighteen or younger. You will never know. Somehow due to some circumstances Siddharth lost control and rammed into a high sidewalk, he was shocked and confused. His nose was bleeding. I didn't even realise what was going around me. Airbags have a thing about them, they can cause serious confusion. We exited the car and tried to calm each other. There was no major damage to the car. Although it did seem like it needed serious body shop work. Siddharth lied down on the footpath and I called a friend of mine. Vijay. He lived nearby and he could reach us the fastest. While Vijay was enroute, I received a message from Meera. I told her everything that had happened. She was willing to give up her anger and come to see Siddharth and I that instant.

I guess that says a lot about her as a person. So Vijay reached the location and we drove to the nearest hospital which turned out to be the same place where Meera had ended up with her friends the night before. We got scanned, we were fine. Let's not go in to the gruesome details. Siddharth and I laughed about how we will never change.

How we started things with good intentions and got into situations like these. We were older and wiser, yes. We were dumber as well.

At 7:00 a.m., Vijay dropped us to Siddharth's place and I left for office. That day itself I had an important meeting, I had to be on my prime. So what do I do? I downed two red bull cans in the Metro. When I reached office I was the most energetic and focussed person there. There I learned two things, everything is a drug if used in the right way. There was a friend of mine, Hari Shankar. Over time, the distance in our friendship grew as he was always very career oriented. I was always great at making friends, I wasn't great at retaining them, because I let people go very easily. I don't crib, I don't beg and I don't say "I miss you." Emotions shouldn't be forced. Romantic or not. I am telling you about Hari because he once told me a story. A story of when he met The Poet. Hari was the president of the drama society of SRCC. The Poet had visited SRCC to "inspire students." When Hari told me about it, it was a rainy day. We were sitting in my car. More like trapped in it. We had a conversation after a long time.

"Bhai, to be an Artist what do you need more? Suffering, love or drugs? Maybe, it's all three who knows." I asked rhetorically.

"Dude, let me tell you a story" Hari smirked.

"The Poet had come to my college and as the society president I was also involved in his hospitality. After the event, we had a conversation for 15 minutes. He told me something that redefined the artist in my eyes."

"Sir, do you think alcohol or drugs has a role in Art?," Hari asked.

"Kid, I used to drink all the time. It would give me amazing movie ideas. I would bring alcohol home every night and get a few sheets so that I can write scripts easily. After I had the first drink, I would decide the genre of the movie. After the second drink, I would decide the names of the character. The third drink, would lead me to place these characters in an emotional setting beyond comprehension. The fourth drink, I would decide the ending of the story. The fifth drink, would help me decide which actors would fit what role. I would write everything down. By the time I would finish the 6th drink, I would fall on the ground and pass out. I would wake up in the morning to be excited about what I wrote. I would pick up the pages to read what I wrote. The pages were blank."

Was this true? Fuck If I know.

I was as amazed of how a person could tell about his deepest darkest nights in such a poetic way to a college kid. Why did I remember this story suddenly? Just like drugs and alcohol don't contribute to art, Red bull doesn't contribute to work. I nailed the meeting but by the time the meeting ended I was so unfazed to know what was happening.

Maybe it was the concussion, maybe it was the constant vomiting or maybe it was that I hadn't slept even for an hour. Just like The Poet hadn't written anything on the paper when he woke up, I would get a feeling of eternal doom after the Red Bull effect wore off. Since, the meeting had ended I was thinking about Meera and how she was angry at me. It was subtle but it wasn't unjustified.

I would probably drive from Delhi to Kupwara if she needed me without a doubt. That's what scares me.

So, I called Meera.

She asked me, "How are you now?"

"Cool, cool, cool, cool," replied yours truly.

I wasn't cool.

She was angry at me. It was clear why. Like you, my reader, she believed that I was judging her. I wasn't. I don't think there would be a time in my life I would judge Meera. It was funny in another universe how I rushed for her and instead of the much deserved love, I was getting the much deserved hatred.

Love is weird. Maybe that's why I appreciate it so much. It's weird and hurtful but it's true.

"Do you really think I went with them because it was a jaguar?"

"No, Meera. Never." I don't know why I had this love for her where I just wanted to look her in eyes and tell her that she was the last person who I would think about in this way. That I can't hold her in that regard, I don't even hold myself in that regard.

"Do you see yourself, Abeer?!"

"What about me Meera?"

"I don't know. Pata nahi! I can't talk about everything on the phone call."

"When can you meet me?"

"I don't know!"

"Okay."

She was angry. Justified. I was fazed out. Justified. We cut the call. I went back to my desk, worked without a hint of anything on my face. Life was tough as a working guy, in love with a girl who was worth everything, while living with his family where he constantly had to make them feel happy. How do you make anyone happy when you aren't happy yourself? Tell them everything you'd want to hear from someone. Tell them you love them and that's enough.

I called her again. I didn't want to be angry at her.

"Hi, Jonu." Jonu was Meera's nickname.

"Abeer, are you okay?"

"Yeah, what could ever happen to me?"

"I don't know. You don't sound okay."

I wasn't. I called her after I vomitted the 5th time that day. I couldn't stop working because if I did I would feel like shit.

She wanted to meet me. So did I. Somehow, after a tiring or a fruitful day, you want to meet someone specific.

We met. We had dinner. We laughed, we made up. More like, she understood what I meant when I explained it to her. She was wise like that. I was random and energetic. She balanced me out and it was worth everything.

I said a lot of things that I shouldn't have. Like how I felt I had a hole in my heart but not around her.

Hole in hearts have a thing about them, the physical ones are rare to find but the psychological ones they are pretty common. I didn't want to tell her what my life was in my own perspective because it was more like an uncomfortable dream. Where I was working, struggling, doing things for other people while not asking anything of anyone. Dear reader, start asking things of people you love. They won't know what you want. I couldn't ask of Meera what I wanted from her, I wanted everything we had and more. I wanted to hold her hand, kiss it, I wanted to look her in the eyes and tell her how beautiful she was and be with her like there was no tomorrow. I bet she had heard all this in her life too. There was nothing I could tell Meera that was new. I can't manage new. All I could manage was the truth. I told her, "There is no version of this where you end up with me." I didn't know that for a fact. Assumptions and expectations are the only two things that could very easily fuck your world up. Learn the subtle art. This is a self help book.

On my way back from her place after 39 hours of no sleep there was only one thing I could understand. This book was coming to an end. I didn't know what I would do about it. I had another anxiety attack. I texted Siddharth, "Bhai call. Please. Abhi." My hands were shaking. My eyes were tearing up, my heart was sinking. I did what any stupid fuck would do, I didn't cry. I wish love could heal everything. No one called, no one texted. This is why I talk to depressed individuals, so that they don't go through something like that. At least not alone. Like I told you, my reader, Meera had her own luggage she didn't need mine. All she needed was love and happiness. I had told Siddharth on Saturday night, "Dude, life is not exciting anymore. It's just office and home. " In the span of this one weekend, I had felt every emotion I could possibly feel. Intense hatred, disappointment, euphoria, fear of dying and unquestionable love (for family, friends and her).

I saw a girl on a cornerstone. She was only her look-a-like. I went in for a closer look, and kissed whoever was sitting there. She was close, she held me very tightly till I asked awfully politely, "please, can I call you, her name?"

Look the lyrics up. My gift to you, my reader.

•••

Weekender: Day 1

Cinema would have you believe that there are miracles bound to happen when you visit a music festival. Be it Bollywood or Hollywood, there is always a time in a movie when the protagonist and their love interest head to a concert, that's where they're gonna fall in love. Movies like 21 and over would have you believe that you meet all kinds of people at concerts and everyone is friendly as fuck. I wouldn't say this isn't true because as you know, cinema can be accurate sometimes too. "Don't watch Bollywood, anymore." said Siddharth. "Bollywood would have you believe in all kind of miracles where you're gonna fall in love with a girl no matter what comes. It's not like that. In actuality, Love has always been just about comfort. If people are comfortable together, they fall in love and maintain the relationships till the moment they don't. Their priorities change, their mindsets change and most importantly they themselves evolve into new human beings which is not necessarily a bad thing. It's a great thing for them, going through a transformation but in that process their partner gets left behind. Break the chain and evolve." Now, you my reader may or may not relate with that but that isn't my concern. My concern is if you go through a similar position someday you'll know what to do. The art of knowing the right time to quit things is essential to lead a happy life. You don't have to prove yourself to anyone.

Did I tell you about a girl that almost ruined me? I let her ruin me. It wasn't her fault, she just had a thing for materialistic and presentable things. I wasn't either of them. I only judged people on the basis of how they treat other people. Nothing else. I was getting in and out of relationships with this particular girl for almost three years. Let's call her, Damini. Damini had a thing about her. Damini didn't put others before herself but she had the entitlement to expect people to do all they could for her. Somehow, I fed that ego. I was a downright beta male. Agreeable, ineffective and lacking a set of balls. She took me along for a ride. Made out with me. Maybe she actually did care at some point, but we'll never know. It doesn't matter. Through coincidence I got to know while she was hooking up with me, she was also looking for a steady partner. I couldn't blame her. Everyone wants to settle down. It's just that her psyche commanded her to look for someone that she could appreciate and respect, that according to her was not me. She was right. I wasn't well dressed most of the times, I didn't socialise much, I disrespected people to feed my insecurities and most importantly I didn't have ambition. After breaking contact with her, I had time to re-evaluate what I wanted and how do I get it. I didn't need a girlfriend, I needed ambition and hard-work. That's what I did. I followed through with my promise to me. I started dressing better, listening and appreciating people and most importantly I started working hard at University. Two years after that, I have a steady workplace, great friends, a loving family and Meera by my side. I honestly couldn't ask for anyone better because no one made me happier.

What was the lesson here? The lesson wasn't that you shouldn't love someone with your whole heart. It's okay to love someone with your whole being. It's beautiful actually. It's that I liked Damini so much, I forgot to work on myself.

I didn't even like myself. That's where it went wrong. To all the people with insecurities, it's okay. One day, you'll be the person you love.

Now, because of this whole experience what I needed from Meera was reassurance. That this won't happen again. Maybe because casual relationships are why our life had reached a down. We were creatures of passion and security at the same time. We would do what we love but we needed something stable to anchor us. That's what I thought at least.

I knew for a fact Meera did a lot for her ex-partner and I didn't want to bring it up. It made her sad. It made me as sad. I had thought that she was not interested in me. That's what she used to say. I guess my therapist was right, people do say things they don't want to say a lot of times.

What I am going to tell you is nothing exceptional. Nothing that wouldn't happen to a lot of people. Nothing that would make you feel a bright light in your chest or cold winds of hell in the back of your neck. It is just a series of events. Take it as such.

Let me start from the very beginning, I am not sure if I've told you this before but Meera and I planned to go to NH7 Weekender, Shillong together. We met at Guwahati airport and planned to move forward to Shillong in a vehicle arranged by a friend of mine. What was expected to be a drowsy late night drive turned out to be a sight to see. All we could see above us were stars. She just kept looking at them and I at her. I loved how excited she was for everything and how her eyes had this glimmer that maybe there was hope for me. By the time we reached the camp we loved everything about it already. Personally, its location was the Unique selling point for me. We talked, clicked pictures, went to the washroom and came back to the tent. We had a sky full of stars, a bottle full of vodka and two livers waiting to be diseased.

So we drank, laughed and talked. The usual gig. It was cold, the tent was small and cuddling was the way to do things right. Since, Meera wasn't my girlfriend I had to think twice before the smallest gestures since it could be taken in very wrong ways. So, I suppressed my thoughts yet again and went to sleep. "Staying around her is a lot of self-control, damn."

The next morning, I woke up way after Meera did. She was a curious one. I was a lazy one. We walked down to have some breakfast. She went to the washroom since breakfast was taking time. I saw a girl next to me smoking a cigarette. Now, I don't smoke anymore. I don't know why I wanted to smoke so much in Shillong. Maybe it was the rock and roll vibe. Leather Jackets, Broken dreams, empty bottles and lit cigarettes.

"Do you want to share that?" I asked her.

"Sure." She replied.

"Where are you from?" Taking a puff of her cigarette, I asked her.

"Kolkata, and you?"

I laughed.

Somehow, I had guessed already she was from Kolkata. If you observe someone properly, you can know lot about them. I really just wait to be surprised most of the time. So we talked and talked. Meera came back.

I introduced Meera to her. Somehow they had talked before. Meera was going to share the tent with her before I was involved in the trip.

Her name was Polo. The Calcutta girl. She was a decent kid. Sweet, innocent, trusting and most importantly kind. We talked for the rest of the morning that day. Just lying down on for the rest floor and talking about things we would rather not. Somehow the conversations were more fun with Meera involved. Wasn't the world more fun with Meera involved? The thing remained, Polo thought we were a couple. I tried to tell her otherwise but Polo was adamant that stuff was going down between us. Maybe it was. Who had the time to think about it?

We were too busy enjoying each other's company. We wouldn't realise when we held hands, when we were talking like we have known each other forever. Now that I think about it I can never comprehend the fact that I've known Meera for only 4 months. Meera, Polo and I bitched about people who click selfies, people who show off their lives on social media and how the world was somehow less romanticised now. I would do what Meera would ask me to do and Meera would do things I never even had to ask her to do. Meera somehow always knew what I needed. We coloured Polo's hair green. Meera wanted to take a walk and so she went off.

Polo and I parted ways too. There was one place I would be at that point. In my tent, with a book, I sat down and started reading my book. So lost in it, I didn't realise it had started raining. Meera came back to the tent.

She asked me, "Do you need your me time?"

"Not really", I replied.

"Good."

Something happened that made my day a bit better than it already was. Meera let out a mild smile. She just took off her shoes and lied down with her head in my lap. I couldn't help but play with her hair. She brought her hand up and held mine. It was so peaceful. For what seemed to be ten minutes, we just looked at the world from our open tent door. I let a breath in and realised, "A trip, Meera and Rock music. The perfect life." The rest of the day just went by smoothly. Then came the evening. The days in our camp were about peace, the environment, love and other drugs. The nights instantly were leather jackets, rock music, parties and other drugs. We got dressed up and left for the concert.

In the bus which was meant to take us to the concert, I met three distinct groups. Cliche guys, The Weed Threesome and Sex-pistols. Cliche guys were a group of college kids whom I met due to the shared affinity to Meghalayan weed. The weed threesome was a guy and two girls who approached me looking for some OCB. Meera didn't believe how I attracted drama. The Sex Pistols were two sexed up couples who seemed like they would fuck anywhere first chance they get. Never befriend people on trips expecting long term friendships. People are a lot different when they travel and when they are in their personal surroundings. In every trip you have made on the basis of Drugs or Alcohol, you can always find these three groups if you look hard enough.

These are the three standard instincts of people on trips. Drugs with friends, drugs with girls and couples who just want to fuck out of the confines of their comfortable home lives.

Meera and I were more like lost souls who found a safe haven with each other in a world that was burning and keeping together simultaneously. All I needed was her by my side.

I don't think you'll find a couple of people like us in a trip easily. We reached the concert, we kept drinking alcohol till rock music hit us.

The first stage that we visited was kind of a bummer. Some couple was up on it fusing rock music with trance. It was weird to be honest. Meera pretended to like it for my sake. I did the same for her sake. Then we decided to bail and drink a lot more. There was nothing profound about the whole experience. You have the rest of the book for profound stuff. We were just being drunk kids in what seemed to be love. If not love, intense affection. It was almost time for the poets of the fall to perform. We entered it with her hand in mine. In another I had a cigarette. A Cigarette, Meera, Rock music and a sky full of stars. Again, Haminastu.

Then came a song, a song that I would grow to love again and all I could see there was how excited Meera was. She would look at me and tell me to concentrate on the stage. Such an idiot. I just hugged her and gave her a kiss on the cheeks. A proper kiss would've been way out of my jurisdiction but one thing wasn't, I held her hand. Both of us looked up at one point on the same time. Stars. Before that point I never understood why she seemed sort of sad when she looked at the stars. "I miss my dad when I look at the stars." She said. And I just hugged her. A part of me wanted to make all of her pain go away but like a lot things that wasn't in my power. Although, I could tell her this. "It's okay. It's all gonna be okay. We are gonna look at stars together later. Now is the time for music." She held my hand and looked at me with that excited look in her eyes. Her excitement made me excited. We danced. The group of guys I was smoking up with were going to hop to another stage. We joined them. She took my hand and took me all the way there. I don't remember the way to the concert. All I remember is she either tripped on a guy who was sitting or she stomped on his leg. Either ways it was pretty funny.

Concerts have certain elements to them which remain constant. They are filled with love, rage, passion, companionship and at the same time a lot of creeps. An old guy would come to Meera and repeatedly kiss her hands and talk to her. I would probably kick his ass. I just stood between him and Meera as making a scene would be the last thing she would want. People would laugh about the #metoo movement every chance they are given until it happened to someone they loved the shit out of. That's us. Human beings. Selfish to such extents that we could only see what was in front of us. What was happening to us.

After the show ended we lied down on the ground looked at the stars and I asked her, "Why do you miss your dad when you look at the stars?" She looked at me in her signature painful expression. The expression in which she wants to look serious and strong but overtime I had learnt it was the face she would choose to hide pain with. Like whenever I want to hide something I just say, "Yeah, I am good. What would ever happen to me?"

"When we were little kids, my sister and I would take dad to the terrace to watch the stars with us. That would make us so happy.

We used to live in Faridabad. Light wasn't such a steady thing to find back then on a place like Delhi. I bet you were a toddler back then." She said. It was a beautiful story. Beauty has a thing about it. It drifts away faster than ugliness.

Pick any instance in your life, the beautiful part just felt like an instance. The ugly part feels like an eternity.

Once upon a time, there was a farmer's boy who was approached by a king. "How long do you think is an eternity?" The king threw a rhetoric at him.

The farmer's boy smiled and said, "There is a hill made of diamonds. It is a 1 mile in every direction. Once in every hundred years, a bird comes and sharpens it's beak on the hill. When the hill is gone, you will know that one second of infinity has passed."

That's what it felt like. Her pain being the constant part of her head. I could only assume a girl who was so loving and affectionate to a guy she had only known for three months. The amount of love she had for deceased parents must've been selfless to the extremes. There was nothing about her that could draw me away from her. Everything just made me hold her hand, hug her tight, smell her hair and kiss her neck. I realised one thing at that point of time. We don't choose the love we deserve. We deserve the love we choose.

I chose her love and it was way better than anyone else ever offered me. I would rather be stuck in the middle with her than be in unquestionable love with someone else. Eternity didn't seem like a long time around her. It was 12 am The day had ended.

•••

Weekender: Self Control is a Virtue

The same night of the first day of concert, when we went back to the camp we just sat by a bonfire. She was hungry so we grabbed some food. There was a portion of time where both of us would be silent and it would be one of the most peaceful times of my life. I just lied down next to her. She had her focus on getting all the heat from the burning fire. My focus lied on the melancholic coldness of the clouds above me and the stars they were covering. Now whenever I would look at the stars I would think of her. How she looked up amidst a concert and said, "I miss my dad when I look at the stars." She said it with a smile on her face and tear drop going down her cheeks. That's what love is. Simultaneous happiness and torment. Looking at the stars I just covered myself with my jacket like a blanket and slept. I don't know how much later it was but Meera woke me up.

"Let's go to the tent. Let's sleep." She said. So we did. It was hard maintaining distance from her knowing my heart would be at peace if I could just hold her and sleep. Restraint is a virtue. We slept immediately I guess.

I had a dream that night. Maybe it was the alcohol and cigarettes. In that dream, I was taking Meera to meet Siddharth. When I met Siddharth, I introduced Meera to him and all he could say was, "There is no one standing there." When I looked towards her, she wasn't there. I rushed out to look for her. She was looking at me with the eyes she had whenever she talked about her parents, her ex or how she was done with love. I just didn't want her eyes to be that sad. I rushed in to hug her and she stopped me. She was unreachable. She was unreal. She was sad. I had solutions for her only if she'd let me. Only if she'd let me heal her and let someone else who hurt her, not hurt her anymore. Whenever she'd tell me about her ex, I would get pretty down and angry. Not because I was jealous or sad. Not because they had been intimate. It was because she went to crazy extents for someone who didn't deserve it. She still was doing that. It was her decision to make. We should all make our own mistakes.

I heard her voice, "Abeer, wake up." I woke up like I usually do. Taking heavy breaths. I had gotten myself checked on multiple occasions. There was not a physical aspect to it. Every time I woke up it was like waking up from the dead. That's why I hated sleeping. Waking up was always hard. So I looked around. She was looking at me. Her face expressionless as my mind were thoughtless. It was the first time I just wanted to kiss the hell out of her because I was just glad she was there.

"What happened?" She asked me. Looking a bit worried.

"Nothing."

I didn't think much I just went in to hug her, cuddle up as well as I could and hold her hand. All I could think of then was how beautiful she was and I am glad she is real. How amazing her hair smelt?

"How can someone like her exist? How can I feel so good around someone?"

I wanted to sleep again. It wasn't the time to do that. I walked out of the tent, walked to the tea shop, grabbed a cigarette and waited for tea. I took two cups and walked back to the tent. I kept the cups outside the tent and went in. Cozied up with her again. I guess it felt like a safe space. I was never scared of anything in my life until I met her. Now, I was scared that I would drown but at the same time something told me she will pull me back out. She was at the same time my pain and my salvation. Isn't that what love is? I just knew a fact that if this was not just a trip but we were actually a thing now, I would feel better. Why? I would know that this could hold. This is not another dream I would wake up from.

Dreams are not good for health. Good or bad. If you have an amazing dream, you will be sad when you wake up because it wasn't true. When you have a bad dream, it's just a bad dream.

The same day we went to a field. A field so beautiful that it almost felt like that's what heaven must look like. Sunlight reflecting on the grass which had a yellowish hint on solid green. Meera, standing there talking about things that meant a whole deal to her. How her friend's ex died and Indigo didn't let her take an off day. How her another work friend's mom was sick and the Manager called her to the office anyways to "confirm" the situation. That's the professional environment I would hate to be in. Either hire people you trust or don't. Don't keep doubting people who work their asses off for you on a daily basis leaving behind their family and social life. Somehow after that conversation we talked about us. What were we? We lied down on the field next to each other looking at the sky and I just brought up the conversation. I don't remember the details of what we said or did but after that conversation I had lost all hope that there was anything between us. Maybe I blocked it out of my mind intentionally who knows? We walked back to the camp and I couldn't help but click her again and again. This was the second time I didn't know what to say to her. I didn't know what to say to myself. I just had a question for life, "How can two people be so similar and so different at the same time? How can one of them feel like this is meant to be and the other one think it's just a phase?"

All I knew this trip was an rollercoaster of emotions. On the way to the concert we had filled up what was left of the vodka in a bottle of a Mango drink. I decided on the way, "Abeer. Bitch. Don't think about this is a rendezvous with what seems to be the love of your life. Think about it the way it is. Think about it as a cigarette, rock music and alcohol rushing in the blood stream along with adrenaline." I got my face on. I was ready to focus on some music. With all this going on in my mind, I totally forgot about the alcohol I was carrying with me. How it had 120 ml vodka in it. How it was full. During the check, the guard told me I can't take it in to the grounds. Logical concern.

The seal of the bottle was broken. Meera was nowhere to be seen. I made the wise choice. I downed it in front of the guard and threw the bottle in trash. The satisfaction that man had in his eyes from what I did. It was like people on opposite sides of a battle with a mutual love for alcohol.

Then I got drunk, obviously. I asked Meera to get on my wavelength so we bought more drinks. So now she was drunk too. We didn't attend one concert for one single reason.

After what happened to her last night with the creepy uncles and unknown gropers I couldn't put her at even 1% of risk. I wasn't that well either to take care of her. So, we just sat in the smoking area and I smoked while she communicated a lot of things. I went to the washroom and when I came back she was smoking a cigarette too. I love women who smoke because they don't have a great regard for life, like me. Meera's smoking was something else. I didn't want her to smoke because she was this bright light that shouldn't be addicted to the likes of nicotine. So I tried to tell her that it's okay if she smoked but it would be great if she didn't make a habit out of it. She was having fun and it was all good. Somewhere between mouth fagging and asking a random dude to teach her how to make rings, she was enjoying as much as she could. So I just stayed close to prevent any misadventure but let her enjoy her time as well as she could. What happened next, she felt a bit sick. So I took her to the washroom where I asked a decent lady to take care of her in there. She helped us out a lot. I smoked with her husband outside the ladies washroom discussing the shows that were being played and missed. It was all worth it as long as Meera was safe and well. She came out and made a baby face, "I want some water." I wanted to laugh, but I didn't as she would think I was making fun of her. I couldn't help but wonder how could someone look so beautiful, brilliant, cute and hot at same time. How looking at someone could trigger the need to observe, respect, cuddle, kiss and preserve at the same time.

So, naturally the drunk ass woman sat down on the ground.

"Water." She demanded.

There were some ladies standing a foot away from her, I asked them to keep an eye on her while I get some water. They were kind enough to help. So, Meera and I drank some water. Got fairly sobered up.

Then came a guy at the spot.

"Why are you guys sitting here?" He asked. "Don't you know there is a concert to attend? Multiple ones actually."

"Yeah, we do Abeer." Meera exclaimed. The childish excited look in her eye came back.

I had to take a tough decision and say no to her. She wasn't exactly alright till that point. The guy got us more booze. I drank her share too. Proud of it.

Then something happened that shouldn't have happened. The guy in his drunken-ness says, "Hoes, Man. They make us miss stuff like concerts too."

Now my reader, I told you about how my face changes at times due to even a slight out of line comment by some idiot. Some line that shouldn't be crossed.

My jaw tightened, my fist closed. I turned to him.

"Apologise, motherfucker. That's no way to talk about her."

We made eye contact and he knew what I meant.

Meera, steps in. "It's okay, Abeer."

"No, it's not." I say not looking away from the face of the guy who massively stepped out of line.

He says, "I am sorry. That was uncalled for, I won't say something like that ever again."

Then I let it be. I actually told him it's okay since he was drunk but it shouldn't happen again. He understood that. So he did what any classic guy would do. While I was distracted, he said something about me to Meera that she didn't like. She just sobered up a lot more and asked me if we could leave. We did. I wouldn't fight a dude just because he was jealous of the company I had, could I?

Meera, took my hand while walking away and hugged me tight as soon as were alone again. I couldn't help but kiss her neck repeatedly. She asked with a shaking voice, "How much do you love me?"

"I don't know." I said continuing kissing her neck.

We just rushed to the concert. Shankar Mahadevan performing breathless. I saw some guys dancing there. In my pursuit of dancing and having fun, I was alternating between dancing with them and Meera. There was a time when Meera and I, had arms around each other and were jumping, laughing and just looking at each other. Her short hair covering a portion of her hair with her left eye and smile clearly visible. I can't forget that moment even if I want to. I don't want to forget it anyways. So, next thing we know the concert had ended. The last day of concert we had just attended 10 minutes of Shankar Mahadevan's gig. Sad realisation. It was all good as her hand was in mine. I looked at her, she looked at me. I wanted to tell her that as long as she was safe, happy and with me there will always be another concert. There will always be a day that was better than the last one. Always be a night more starry than the previous one. Always a song that was better than the last one.

The guys I was dancing with, they wanted to get pictures clicked. One of them handed Meera the camera and invited me to join them. Meera in her signature form dictated who sits where and does what. I loved her confidence and control over other people's actions. We got the pictures clicked then I asked a stranger to click a picture of all the guy, me and Meera. Meera came and sat with me, taking my hands and wrapping them around her. These small things play well in the heart of a cynical guy like me.

Then I took their leave, I went to Meera who was then standing near by the stage. I went took her waist in my hands, "what's next, miss?" The smile on our faces. We finally had made a trip, attended a music festival, drank down and were satisfied with each other. Such a roller coaster of emotions this trip was. In that moment, it just felt like we were two kids in love all over again. Maybe it was the alcohol, the music, the drama or the environment.

"You can talk to anyone with the same confidence, can't you?" She inquired with a smirk on her face. I love it when she did that. I loved everything she did anyway.

"Yes, Ma'am" It had been a while since I was smug. I can't be the wise idiot all the time.

She pointed out a girl for me in a crowd and said, "Go tell her you love her."

"Cool." I started walking towards her. Now there were multiple times on the same day, that we met a couple in their 40s who were as drunk as us and were falling on slopes again and again. Each time I saw them I exclaimed, "I love you guys" and the husband would naturally say, "I love you guys too."

Looking at them I always imagined that Meera and I would be the same couple. In their 40s drinking our hearts out at music festivals, falling over each other and laughing about it. Maybe me telling the couple that I love them inspired Meera to give me this dare or maybe it was because I was talking to absolutely anyone during the trip.

I turned around to look at her, she was smiling. I asked her, "Do you really want me to do this?"

She let out a sigh and smiled looking down, "No. Come here."

I started walking towards her. I blacked out for a second or two and the next thing I remember. We were kissing each other right there. On the concert grounds with everyone standing around us. Nothing on my mind then, just that how my hand automatically went to her neck and hair. How her hand did the same thing. How it was amazing and not a dream.

She paused and looked at me, "Abeer, will we regret this in the morning?"

I didn't know what to say. Not exactly great at predicting what's gonna happen when it comes to Meera.

"Let's regret it in the morning. Not right now." I said kissing her neck and then back to the lips.

Single malt whiskey on a Monday afternoon. A promise to the heavens.

I had a feeling this was short lived but I didn't care. She says, "Let's stop when I ask you to."

"Yes, Ma'am"

And then she stopped me to ask in a while and I did. We walked back to the shuttle not regretting a thing. We got on the bus to find seats in the back. There was a lady sitting between us. She was socialising and I was just doing that at the same time holding her hand behind the lady's back and glancing at her beautiful self from time to time. We went back to tents being the only two loud people on a bus full of tired people. Classic Delhi Behaviour. Loved it.

When we reached the tent, she immediately slept. I didn't want to sleep then. I went to see Polo. She and I decided to go get some tea. We sat near an abandoned bonfire and I told her everything that happened. The kid was wise. She told me a few things I already knew. All I had to do was think less and be more patient. Then I went ahead and slept in the tent. It was 1 am

"Abeer." Said Meera shivering in her bean bag. It was 3 am I was worried about her. I just immediately hugged her and rubbed her back. She was still cold. We went out to sit near a bonfire. She needed all the heat she could get. The Weed Threesome found me. Offered me some drugs and alcohol. I was only young, old, sad and excited at the same time. How do I say no to Drugs and Alcohol in a jungle party? Cliché guys found me next and invited me to dance with them. So I did. Meera approved. She was sitting near the bonfire and I was dancing with some guys on random music. I would take breaks and look at her to find out that most of the times she would be looking at me too.

I would take a break go put my head in her lap talk to her and go back to dancing when a song I like would come on. I danced till the sun came out. Meera and I decided to go to our spot to watch the sun rise.

That's where I asked her to keep this thing going. That kissing her was way better than not kissing her. I couldn't tell anymore what she wanted. Before the trip, it was that we were two people going to watch a concert. Now it was two people who had come so close in the span of three months that everyone we met thought we were a couple. It just felt like love was like the slender man staring at our faces and that we were two scared kids trying to tell ourselves that it wasn't so. The thing is kids, Abeer doesn't assume. Abeer hates when he is let down. So he blocks out such feelings. Maybe it was actually a moment that happened as she described it. She didn't strike me as someone who would have a moment with someone she didn't care at least a bit about. Life is a creature who feeds off on people's shortcomings. Meera didn't like me. I loved the hell out of her.

We went back to the tent. I had decided not to cuddle up with her anymore. It would only hurt me. Self control is a virtue. I closed my eyes off for five minutes and I woke up because of a nightmare again. Breathing hard to find some oxygen. She knew what it was about. I couldn't help but put my arms around her and hold her hand. I couldn't sleep anymore. It was five am My nose buried in her neck, taking in her smell that was flawless like everything about her. She turned her face to me and slept. It was hard not kissing her at that point.

Self control is a virtue. So, I kissed her.

She did too. Instant electricity rushed through our bodies.

Her lips, my lips. Apocalypse. Then it came again.

"Stop, Abeer. This doesn't feel right." She shivered a bit.

"Is it because I am twenty-two?" I was curious, a bit shocked and happy.

"No, idiot." She laughed. "You just feel it in your gut. What's right and what's not."

It was unreal. How does she not feel what I feel? Is it so one sided? Is it time to take a step back. Self control is a virtue. Loving Meera a rollercoaster.

Then something happened to her. She got up. Panicked a bit. Her body shaking like mine did under anxiety. Meera told me she suffered from anxiety but she didn't tell me it was this serious.

I was scared. I didn't know whether to hug her or to give her space. I went with my gut. I gave her space. She went outside, brushed her teeth, washed her face and came back. She was talking about what we had to do (what we had to pack and what we had to do) and I was just looking at her.

"Come here." I told her.

She looked at me and came into my arms. I told her that I was sorry for what happened. I wasn't sorry for kissing her. I was sorry not to ease into it and push her over a line while doing it. It wasn't even about making out. It was about her. I would not kiss anyone else given the circumstances. She was not replaceable. I always believed that in this world everyone is replaceable.

As soon as she let go, I wondered. "Am I replaceable?" Fuck if I know.

•••

The Drive

Packed bags, unfinished cuddles, disappointed faces and righteous attitudes. That's how morning began. It wasn't about what had happened. It was about what was going to. The dream was gone. The trip was over. I didn't know if there was going to be a second one. I didn't know what was in her mind. "Always ask someone rather than assuming." I told myself. We had our breakfast. We had loaded the vehicle and my friend's driver was driving back to Guwahati Airport. We had some quality music around us. That drive she was looking at the scenery and I was looking at her. With a smile as wide as my face. The windows were open, our hair flowing with the fresh mountain air and her face of knowing that someone was observing and adoring the fuck out of her.

"What happened to you today, Meera?"

"I haven't thought about it."

"Are you okay? It just felt right. You seemed into it too. What happened suddenly?"

"It isn't the first time it has happened, it is not the last."

"Why haven't you thought about it, Meera?"

She looked at me with a death stare and said, "It's your emotions, Abeer. Not mine."

Something shattered in me again but I was mature enough not to be a kid about it again. I took my time, swallowed my pride and continued being the Abeer I was. Thinking about her happiness. Somehow what she had didn't feel real. It felt forced. I didn't pay much attention to this feeling because human beings have a habit of justifying things to ease their pain.

She went to sleep. I started looking out of the window. How Meghalaya was God's own country but nothing could please and unsettled my heart. It's human to be down in the face of rejection. It would be inhumane to hurt Meera over it. I could only hurt Meera when she was wrong. She wasn't wrong. She was playing with the cards she has dealt. It was important to have a talk with her, a talk that decided where we wanted to stand.

I told you about Damini, right? Damini had me her way. She kissed me when she wanted to, fucked me when she wanted to and loved me when she wanted to. She kept me along till she found someone better but isn't that human nature? To want more? I got to know that she would date someone else, had he agreed and I would've been kicked to the curb. That's what love is for most people nowadays, something to pass their time till they find something that's convenient. I didn't want to make the same mistake again. I slept thinking about this.

What was Meera's perspective? She had found someone who cares about her, who makes her laugh, who is a bit demanding and idiotic at times but he means well. He is not a standard gentleman. He is not anything she wants in a partner. Someone she can feel safe with. Someone she can confide in without being judged. Someone who wanted to hear her story.

Maybe in the heat of the concert and living together, she had made the solid mistake of falling for that feeling a bit. Maybe she actually did like me and was scared it would go to shit like everything did before that. Who knows? I try not to assume. All I knew was she looked at me with the same affection and kindness with which I looked at her. Maybe she was scared that I would hurt her too. Love seemed promising and diving into it was easy. Heartbreaks are not a joke. All I knew was I didn't know what either of us would regret more. Giving it a chance or not?

While sleeping in that car, I heard her voice, "Abeer" and I realised she was hugging me. When I asked her what it was about later, she told me she just hugs someone when she wakes up. It's a habit. Sweet, right? Isn't she pretty loveable?

We had reached the airport an hour before we needed to. Grabbing lunch was the practical thing to do. We headed to a restaurant. Nothing had changed. We talked like always we did. I still held her hand and she held mine. It was time for a talk. I told her what was my past experience with Damini. I told her I didn't want that to happen again and that she had to make up her mind. She could take as much time as needed and decide. I never gave her any ultimatums but this is the first time I had to. She always knew what she was doing but I wasn't so sure anymore.

So I just told her, "I will just give you one suggestion. Don't take this decision under the influence of what happened in your past relationships? You are not the same person you used to be. I am not like either of your ex's. I am Abeer. I just truly believe that what's happening to us in natural and is meant to be. Don't spoil something good and natural for something bad and forced that happened a long time ago. If you want time, I'll wait. Without doubt. If you don't want to do this, I'll try to move on. But if you do want to do this, I will love you."

She seemed like she was considering it but I can't say for sure. Who knows what goes in someone's head when it comes to love? She didn't need more pain and confusion in her life and all I wanted to do was take it away. If we were to continue the same path of holding hands, cuddling and kissing each other when it was convenient someday someone's heart would be broken. It would pull us apart like nothing else. At the airport while seeing her off, I hugged her and kissed her on the neck. Was it a habit now? Who knew? After she left, I took out my laptop.

In times like these you have to stick to what you are passionate about. People come and go. Meera and my story would run it's course for as long it was destined to. Focus on things you have control over. Even if you love someone with all your being, you can't control what they feel or do. You shouldn't even try to. Take my advice as someone who is clinically depressed and borderline suicidal. People can't be your redemption, neither can love. Your only redemption can be what you love. So I sat down at the airport, drank a litre of water.

•••

The Wait

Hatred. I never carried much hatred in my hearts for any particular thing or being. I was about to realise the only thing I've hated most in my life is waiting. Point being, aren't all human beings waiting for something? Some of them are waiting for a promotion, for food delivery, for their life to mean something and some are waiting for love like Avicii did (May God bless his soul). I was waiting for Meera's answer. Everything was going great so why did I bring in this thing about love and relationships? Maybe because I wanted to know what to expect. Maybe because love is just love. It's stupid, irresistible and it has to make your life and dick harder. Meera was the least of my problems. Meera was the solution to a lot of problems. Can't sleep? Hold Meera in your arms and take a deep breath. Can't feel a thing? See Meera get excited and smiley over things. Can't enjoy alcohol? Drink with her. It wasn't so that life wasn't possible without her. It was just that life seemed much worse when she wasn't around.

Today was Diwali. The Festival of lights as every kid has described it in their school essays. It's meant to be a beautiful day about love and family. It was grand. I had an amazing time with my cousins, helped my mother make Rangoli and prepare for Puja. All this while doing nothing but enjoying my time. The day has ended and all I wanna do is drive to her place and give her a tight hug and these earrings I bought for her. I have a feeling that would come on a bit strong to her. Also, I bet at this exact point she is either having some alcohol with her adorable family or she is spending time with the cute kitten Hridda. It's a weird feeling, thinking about someone and smiling more than I've smiled at Chocolate Noir Shake from Big Chill Cakery, New Delhi. It's also a weird feeling to miss the shit out of someone. I've always hated sleeping alone. Maybe that's why I don't sleep. Who knows? Now, that I had held her in my arms and napped for mere seconds I just know that it's more peaceful than a Bhakt's mind on seeing a Ram Mandir.

It's the same concept of Man-eating tigers. As soon as a tiger gets a taste of human blood, can't go back to preying on other animals. My affection for her wasn't such an aggressive one but it was similar in one manner, once I got that little glimpse of a life with her, life without her seemed much worse than it used to be. Not all the time, just when I was free. Whenever I was free these days I would remember small details about her from the trip and they would make me brighten up. Let me tell you a few that could brighten you up a bit too. Meera was sunlight in a shit storm for me, maybe she could be one for you too.

It was a chilly night in Guwahati, Meera and I had just landed. We entered our car and we sat facing each other. It seems hard to forget how excited she actually was. I didn't remember the last time I was excited for anything. Maybe that's why I liked having her around me. The pure innocence, excitement and wisdom at the same time. We had our backs against the car door from the inside. We were facing each other and talking. I had full control of the music in the car and as like Delhi's boys like to call it "Gaadi ka DJ." I gave her the phone to put on anything she liked. It was this instance when she got all excited and punched my shoulder with affection, "Abeer, look up." She demanded. So I did. The stars were a sight to absorb but somehow my stupid self enjoyed looking at her while she was looking at them. That smile. I brought down the car window, rested my head on the window with my back against the door and looked up at the sky. It wasn't as beautiful as her excitement. My head was slightly out of the car and she got a bit worried. I asked her to do what I was doing. Sit in the same position and look at the stars. She did. I looked at her with due diligence, stupidity, affection and wonder. Diligence because I was a bit worried that she would get hurt. Stupid because it was then that I realised, I was a stupid kid in love. Affection came naturally with the realisation. Wonder because I bet it was the most beautiful sights I had witnessed. I had been to the deserts of Egypt, the cold mount of St. Catherine, The lavish beaches of Mauritius, The beautiful valleys of Kashmir and Himachal, the serene sunset at Kanyakumari (the end of mainland India), the depths of Mediterranean sea and top of the skiing point at Gulmarg. Yet, my favourite sight to take in was Meera's excitement. In the moment, it would seem that life isn't that worthless anyways.

Maybe there is something called love hanging somewhere around this eternal void. Her hair flowing with the wind, her smile as wide as it could be, a sparkle in her eyes brighter than the brightest star and how life went from Monochrome to Technicolor.

There was a moment in the tent before I kissed her where my face was just buried in her neck and her face was facing the ceiling,

"Are you real, Meera? Is this a dream or is this a cruel joke? How can someone be so flawless?" I asked myself.

"This is all a matter of perspective, Abeer." She'd have replied.

At a point in our car while driving back to Guwahati after the festival had ended, there came on a song which I really liked. It was a Punjabi song. The lyrics of that song was about the same conversation between us where a guy can't stop appreciating the girl and the girl just tells him that it's his perspective. No one should love anyone for all I care. If you do love her, you gotta let her under your skin. Then you begin to make it better. (Yes, another music reference. Sue me.)

At the same time, I had asked her about what happened when I kissed her. Did I do something wrong? I was a bit worried. She told me that she wasn't thinking about it.

Naturally, I asked her "Why?"

It was a genuine question. You'd think about something like that wouldn't you. Am I the weirdo here? Who knows?

To my question she had a heartbreaking response.

"I am not thinking about it because these are your feelings, Abeer. Not Mine." She said with a look in her eye that was so unfamiliar that it didn't even seem like her. I didn't know what to say to that. Naturally, with the hand holding, cuddling, deep talk and a kiss that was pushed by a "moment" I thought maybe we were reaching somewhere. It was either that Meera meant what she said or she was scared and didn't want me to pursue anything. Either ways I didn't want to react or fight. I didn't want to hurt her, I didn't want to hurt myself either. So, I just went to sleep. She had slept too.

The rest of it you know already my reader. I didn't include it in the story maybe because it was either too dark for me to write about then or that I didn't think she was being honest. She said she didn't have feelings for me, her eyes would tell a different story.

I just didn't know a whole big portion of Meera anymore. With more certainties came more uncertainties. Turning out to be a really cliché modern day love story, isn't it?

It was heartbreaking because she had told me once, "If you had met me six months ago, life would've been different. Now, I am just done with relationships. It's too much for me."

She was hurt. I get that. Someone hurt her bad, you know that too. I didn't want to do that. I didn't plan to do it. I couldn't even comprehend to do that. I wanted to preserve and love her like the squirrel from ice age loves the chestnut. Like the love Snoop Dogg has for weed and Nickleback has for mediocre music.

The biggest mistakes one could make in love is not to listen to the other party. More times than not, they are telling the truth. Give them the benefit of doubt. I trusted Meera's instincts as much I trusted mine but they can be wrong sometime too. It could be that this could be the best relationships we could ever know because of the natural ease, trust, bond and friendship.

There is something that never crossed my mind. It does now. I've been born with a silver spoon in my mouth. My family loves me a lot, my friends miss me, money was not an issue, my elder brother sheltered me from the world and I've always had what I wanted. Meera on the other hand, lost her parents, was left heartbroken multiple times and had seen a bad time in terms of money most importantly, how come she saw beauty in everything that came her way and how did I hate everything except my solitude? How come I wasn't happy around my family even though they loved me? How come I didn't want to see my friends more frequently? How come I just wanted to travel and leave everything behind? Was it because I knew my family and friends would be fine without me? Was it because I couldn't be restrained in one place? Was it the reason for my misery? That I wanted to run away but it was my own morality holding me behind? As a kid, I was always the wrong one in the family. My parents still look at me with this certain loving disgust in their eyes. Sort of like, they wouldn't choose to love me if they were given the choice. I can't blame them. Meera on the other hand, even strangers loved her. Everyone adored the hell out of her. She cared for other people more than she cared for herself. I bet she never realised it. I can be that person too. I just don't want to be anymore. It's energy I am not supposed to waste. For all I care, I don't wanna die but I would've been fine if I wasn't born at all. I don't have hatred for anything. I am just indifferent to most things maybe because nothing feels like anything.

I would let you in my psyche more but this isn't about me. It's about her. Loving her like every healthy relationship is constant effort. Like a tree, you have to water all the time to keep it fresh.

Maybe no one wants a tree where I've helplessly planted it. Maybe, watering that tree is the problem not the solution. Too many maybe's.

It is one am after Diwali. She has gone to sleep. I hate how much I want her company but it's okay. I'll be older and wiser someday. It's difficult to comprehend how she doesn't want the same company from Me after the chain of events. Evidence suggests she actually meant what she said in the car that day. "It's your feelings. Not mine." It's just a vicious circle.

People hurting people who love them. Like a food chain. For the first time I thought we would break the chain and be together. Life had played a cruel joke. It had shown me the best I could feel and then it was gone. That's not dark, that's life. I told you it feeds on people's sorrow. I didn't have any, so it got me to a point where I love something and then it was gone. Now I had sorrow on my plate and life wasn't a starving beast anymore. All I could do was wait and see what Meera wanted with me. Either ways it would be okay for me. In the wise words of Rumi, "What you're looking for, is looking for you."

Just one question remained. What would Meera regret more? Taking a chance on love or not taking a chance at all?

•••

The Night All Hell Broke Loose

My dear reader, it's been a while since I've talked to you. Did you think I forgot about you? I've been thinking about you all this while. What you are taking away from this storm of confusion and hopeless love. Do you think I am being played like my overprotective friends do? Do you think I am being stupid? Do you think I am wise? That's debatable. How you would react to someone like Meera would solely depend upon the cards you've been dealt with in life. At this point, she had made it clear that she didn't know what she wanted. She couldn't decide. She wasn't my primary focus anymore. It was my sleep cycle. For months, I wasn't sleeping more than four hours at a stretch. I would either have an unexplainable dream or a revolting nightmare. It hadn't always been like this.

Let me tell you a story. A story that shaped me into the person I am today. Like every bored dude with an internet connection and no love life, I was active on tinder. I matched a few girls on it but they were never appealing. Once, I went to see a girl at an Airbnb she had booked in Gurugram just to hook up for the sake of it. I had never done that. When I entered the room, we smoked a few cigarettes, drank some alcohol and when it came to doing the honours, I made an excuse to run away. I realised one thing that day, I wasn't a hookup person. I am still not. Weeks after this unfortunate event, on one fine night one of my tinder matches called me up. We had exchanged numbers.

"Hi, Abeer. This is Shivangi. I really really need to get out of my house tonight. I am having a really hard time with my family."

"What happened? Is everything okay?" I was worried.

"Can you pick me up? I will tell you when I see you." She seemed desperate.

"Wait let me call you in five."

"Okay."

I called Siddharth and some friends. Told them about the scenario. Asked for his opinion because I barely knew Shivangi. Tinder situations turning dangerous in India are not unheard of. We reached the conclusion that we'll call her to my place, Siddharth would come to my place too and we'll talk to her. So, I invited Shivangi to my place. She was here in say 20 minutes. I tried calling Siddharth but he wouldn't pick up. So, I entertained her. As soon as she entered, her eyes fell on the well decorated bar my father had established with patience and money. We didn't drink as a family, it was just one of the attractions of our house. My family wasn't home that night. So, she picked up a fine bottle of double black and started pouring drinks. She seemed so sad and tired that I didn't say much. If my parents asked where the alcohol went, I would've said I drank it and no one would bat an eye.

As soon as she got drunk enough, she started talking. She told me she was still in high school (12th standard) and she was eighteen years old. (On tinder her age was twenty.)

I checked her ID to be sure of her age. She was eighteen so I let her stay. She started crying and telling me how her father died when she was considerably young. Like I told you my reader, losing a parent is the worst thing I can imagine for someone after being raped. After her father died, her Mama molested her. When she gathered the courage to tell her Mother about it, she asked her to brush it off. To bury the truth. Her mother even went to the length of accusing Shivangi of lying or making it up. Shivangi, was devastated. You could tell by looking at her that she probably hadn't taken a bath for at least a weak. Dirty, unkempt hair. Dark circles. Skin looking as unhealthy as it could. Eyes full of pain.

She then hugged me and cried. I tried to tell her it'll be better. I wasn't sure how someone so young and sweet could get into a mess so deep.

"After all this, I have such low regard for my body that I am drinking at a stranger's place. It wouldn't even make difference to me if you raped me right here." She cried.

It shattered something in me. You know when you see or hear something so heartbreaking that you grow up in an instant.

There was a moment where it felt like she wanted something more to happen between us but honestly, that was the last thing on my mind. I just talked to her. Made her laugh. I am good at that. Feeling like shit and making other people laugh. Even around Meera no matter how much I am shattered on the inside, I make her laugh. I love both of them in their own separate ways now. Shivangi was a kid I wanted to protect. My friends arrived to my place. We sat with her and talked at the dining table. She then told me that she was on medication for clinical depression and bipolar syndrome. I didn't know much then but I knew that it doesn't go well with Alcohol. While telling me this, she just vomitted on the ground and fell on the vomit. My friends and I were so shocked it was almost like a nightmare. We picked up her unconscious self and put her in my bed. We made some home made remedies for her so as to get her sobered up. We were going inside the bedroom every fifteen minutes to check on the kid. We were scared. My friends were panicking since she was a school kid and we were five guys in an empty house with her. God forbid if something bad happened to her, it could take our lives away. I just told them that they should go and I'll handle it. It was my house. She was my responsibility.

At one point, one of my friends went into the bedroom and he came out shouting, "Bhai, she is not breathing. Her eyes are open."

I rushed in, I still remember her face. No expression on it. Blank eyes staring directly at me who was standing on the door. I've seen dead bodies before and it was nothing less. I rushed in, lightly slapped her face. Sprinkled water on her face. She gained consciousness. I was surprised that none of my friends left my side to save themselves. In times like these, you get to know who your real friends are. Saurabhan and I, insisted on dropping her home as soon as she was functioning normally. I was angry and scared. She lied to me. If I had even a whiff of her medications, I wouldn't let her drink. So we drove in silence and dropped her home.

Saurabhan and I were shaking in the car on our way back home, grateful that she was okay and so were we. It's natural to be caring but in a situation like this one tends to think about themselves too. For the next three days, whenever I would think of Shivangi I would vomit. I would cry like a bitch. I was scared to contact her for a while but I did later on.

Some of my friends in the pursuit of lightening up the situation, made a joke out of it. In front of every stranger they would say things like, "Abeer, tell them about the time you were gonna hookup with a school girl who suffered from clinical depression." I told my friends that Shivangi had committed suicide because I didn't want to go through this again and again. It was the darkest chapter of my life. I was still in touch with Shivangi. I tried to talk to her and help her. She would barely listen to a stranger would she. One fine day, I got to know that Shivangi actually killed herself. She jumped off a terrace in Indirapuram. Ironically enough, her colony was enroute Meera's place. Whenever I would go to drop her, I would see Shivangi's place. I didn't want to tell Meera about it because she got spooked easy. She was a strong woman but everyone has a weak point right. I found it cute. There were a lot of things I couldn't tell Meera anymore. Things like how in most of my nightmares till this date I would see Shivangi. How sometimes I am scared to go in my bedroom because I am afraid I will see Shivangi lying in the bed lifeless with her eyes open staring at me. Meera had her battles, I had mine. Who had the right to say who was more traumatised?

The reason Devika and I broke up was because of that happened with Shivangi. She thought I had something going there. Something deep and dark. I was at a point where I wouldn't go around explaining anything to anyone. People assume whatever makes them more comfortable with the truth.

It's November, 2018 and I still can't sleep. Even when Meera is around. Thankfully, she has got her sleep apnea under control and is doing well in that regard. She is in a better place.

There was an incident at my office. One of the interns was caught staring down/ stalking one other woman in a co-working space. It had come to me to decide whether or not to fire him. After multiple attempts, the intern wouldn't change his way. He stalked the girl even outside the workplace. The girl seemed pretty scared and after Shivangi, I had zero tolerance to see some girl scared because of some random guy. So, I fired him. Later, he committed suicide. Another day, another suicide. It blew a fuse in me. Even if I closed my eyes for five seconds, I would see Shivangi. I didn't sleep for three days straight. I didn't tell Meera about my sleep because she wasn't my babysitter. She needed her place of mind. It's difficult being visually depressed around a functional family because if they see even a frown on your face they get worried. If they get worried, they get anxious. Them getting anxious doesn't make things better. I hated how I just wanted to hug the hell out of Meera all this while. Sort of like, how a drug addict needs his fix whenever an issue comes his way. So, I took the difficult way. I tried to fix things by myself. I did fix a fair share of it.

On one fortunate Friday, I was so tired of acting happy and well for my family that I took my car and went out on a drive. CP was my destination. I parked my car in front of Nando's. It was a beautiful winter evening. I put my phone on DND. I just walked and walked. Looking at the happy kids with balloons, happy middle aged couples sharing ice cream, happy young couples smoking cigarettes and groups of friends walking out of bars happy and drunk.

I drank a litre of water and sat near Palika Bazaar. There were two guys with three guitars jamming. I joined them.

We sang songs of heartbreak and all I could think of was Meera then. It didn't feel like my heart was broken then and there but it could be very easily by life. Life is a creature who preys on the weak. We just sat in a park singing "Kun Faaya Kun" for thirty minutes. I had planned to meet Meera at 8:30 p.m. I was a bit sleepy then so I grabbed some coffee from a Starbucks and sat near the Janpath crossroads. I sat on a cornerstone.

That's when a girl came and sat right next to me. These days, I wouldn't be surprised if it was some random girl wanting to start a conversation. Shit like that was happening a lot with me these days. I was in no mood to entertain a strangers. I looked at the girl, she was beautiful. Short hair, beautiful eyes and lips like whiskey on a Monday afternoon. It was Meera. She had seen me sitting there. She knew about the intern. We talked. Somehow, still feeling like shit I made her laugh. I guess that came naturally to me. She made me laugh, too. She made me genuinely happy.

It's funny how just talking to some selected people can make you feel a lot better. I didn't have to pretend in front of her. We were just two mental health patients trapped in a movie.

She was hungry. So, we went to Al Kausar near Assam Bhawan. (Amazing Tundey Kebab). We didn't know where to head to next. There was a place that still felt like home. I never thought I would ask her to go there after all this while.

"Do you wanna see the place where I grew up?" I asked nervously.

"Yes. Whatever you want." She said with a smile as bright as the sun would shine if there was not the prominent smog in Delhi.

We went to Pragati Vihar Hostels, Lodhi Road. It was a colony with quarters with one bedroom each. We weren't as economically well then as we are now. Life was way simpler. Siddharth and I were teenage rebels on a quest to checkout girls, eat ice-creams at night and Chole Bhature for breakfast. Whenever he would breakup with someone he would come sit with me on the staircase near my house. Times were better. We didn't need alcohol to have a good time. We would eat chips sitting on the terrace.

My home was still as simple and as beautiful as ever. Like a tour guide at a heritage site, I told Meera about every incident and where it happened with the excitement of when I was a kid who lived there. I showed her Jasleen's house. My long lost friend.

I showed Meera where I went for tuition. Where I sat when I wanted to bunk and play video games. During all this I didn't realise how I was holding her hand and how there was feeling of satisfaction in my chest in a long long time. Meera and I, went to all these places without second thoughts. Nostalgia has a thing about it, it's better when you share it with someone you love the fuck out of. It was also a gentle reminder of when my family didn't have much but was knited together closely. Four people living in a one bedroom apartment. My mom used to cook and do all the chores. My brother used to lazy around without second thoughts or regrets. My father was sometimes frustrated given our financial condition but I was happy because it was home. I could always step out and see all my friends. I could always go to the spot on the terrace where I could see Jawaharlal Nehru Stadium at it's prime.

This spot on the roof is where Siddharth and I drank together for the first time. Where we each of us kissed our first girlfriends.

Where we would run off to when families were being hard. It was a place where we dreamt of life being life. Nothing more, nothing less.

When I took Meera there (the spot on the roof) for the first time, I could see the wonder in her eyes too. It wasn't just me. It wasn't just sweet nostalgia. That place was made of dreams. Meera and I stood there together laughing, talking, absorbing the view and adoring each other. That's when we started discussing the kiss we shared after the concert. I enacted the whole thing because she was a bit drunk and she couldn't stop laughing.

"Come here." I told Meera in the same way she did at the concert.

She came near me with a smile on her face.

"Abeer, this could go very wrong." She said.

"Fuck it." I said with the confidence that life couldn't go worse than it had. It was the four month anniversary of Shivangi's death, my intern had just died and I hadn't slept for three days.

We kissed yet again.

We loved it.

She pushed back again.

"No, Abeer. We're not doing this."

Love is love.

Confusion is confusing.

"Self control is a virtue." I told myself, hugging her. She laughed.

We left the place. It was 11:10 pm. It was time to drop her home. While driving, I was a bit flirty and talkative because she wasn't. I was consumed by the thought of the suicides around me and I didn't want that to radiate to Meera. For example whenever I feel like I am in love, I purposely listen to fuckboy music. It helps mellow down the love. Too much love is hard to digest for anyone. My thought process was filled with uncertainties on the why and the how, I was avoiding my feelings. Why do I do this to myself every time? Is it because I didn't want to bum anyone out? So I started sharing.

I told her what I felt and she had all the right answers because of the beautiful and smart person she is. At this point of time, Meera was not on a pedestal of love. She was just Meera, I was just Abeer. I had seen her imperfections and they didn't matter. All that mattered was I wasn't depressed around her.

When I saw, Shivangi's house I held Meera's hand. I didn't let her know what it was about. Since, I was driving an automatic car my left leg and hand was pretty much free. I wanted to scream but I rather put up a smile. Meera didn't have a solution to this. It was my weight to bear. Meera didn't have solutions to my problems but she was there when she was needed. Always. Without doubt. Trying her best with the cards we were dealt by life. I wanted to tell her, "You met me at a very strange time in my life." Like in the movie Fight Club. I had a feeling she would say the same thing to me.

We sat in my car outside her house. It was 11:40 p.m. We talked and I wanted to kiss her again. I got selfish. I lost control. Self control is a virtue that I have always had, just not anymore. My father would be proud.

"Can I kiss you again? I wouldn't ask if it was not today."

"Oh so you won't ask again?" She asked with her mischievous little smirk.

"Oh I will if need be." I said dazed and confused.

She took off her specs, so did I. And we face battled. I don't want kiss to be the most common word in my book so we will call it a face battle at some points now.

It was beautiful while it lasted.

"no. no. no. no. NO!!" Meera said pulling back while pushing me back.

"We can't keep doing this. Abeer, we won't kiss again it just triggers something in me.

She was sobbing and shaking. I hugged her and told her I wasn't going anywhere. I was right here. It's fine. My body holding back a panic attack of my own. Two patients in a quest for something like love.

It was heartbreaking to see her so vulnerable. We shared something beautiful and it had this effect on her. I couldn't see her like that regardless of the cost. So, I did what felt right. After she calmed down, we talked. I hugged her goodbye. I asked her to do me a favour and think about what had happened. I knew for a fact that ignoring your anxieties only increase them. Like Single Malt whiskey on a monday afternoon, the kiss didn't end well either. That's just life. In other cases, quite frankly I would see myself as the victim. Now I saw myself as the perpetrator.

On my way back, I saw Shivangi's house again. I said Goodbye. Drove as fast as I could without it being a danger to anybody. All I could think about was Meera's face saying when she pulled back and sobbed, Shivangi's face when she was lying on my bed like a corpse and my intern's face when I had fired him. All the faces of people I had failed. Somehow I at the same time felt intense love for the people and intense hatred for the circumstances. Maybe I was being too hard to Meera. All I wanted was to love her and be loved. Maybe it was too much to ask at this point of time? Maybe in my own struggles, I had ignored her's. My reader, I am not a role model. I am just a twenty-two year old guy trying to be a better human being, waiting to love a girl who has developed a certain repulsion to the feeling.

I don't have the answer to my problems as of now, my friend. I will someday. Will I share them with you? Hell, yes.

When I reached home, I talked to my brother. He was stressed and I tried to help him out of it. We agreed on one thing, It was 2:00 a.m.

I fell on my bed and went in to a deep dreamless slumber. Have you ever had so much to worry about in your life that you just go to sleep?

Sort of like when your house is burning in all directions and all you can do is sit and wait? That was life now.

•••

The Therapist: Is This Real Life?

Hi, There is something on my mind. Something that I hid from you. My first therapist was fuck-all. I think both of us agree on that. Money minded, treacherous and opportunistic. Basically, I would rather get a nose full of cocaine like Mia Wallace than visit her again. Nevertheless after the dilemma I needed someone to help me with my issues. So, I started searching for someone else who could help me clear my thoughts. Someone, qualified enough. Someone not opinionated. My brother was helped by a therapist when he was going through a down point. Sometimes I think we are a bit privileged to have conditions like depression and anxiety. Most people around us had struggles like poverty and starvation. We were doing well in our careers, our family was loving and our friends had always been there. I didn't know the root of our dysfunction. I didn't know why we had the same conditions. What helped me the most was not ignoring my problems. What helped me the least was thinking of my problems as mere bumps in the road. Keep that in your dumb little mind, reader.

So, I contacted his therapist. I knew for a fact that she wasn't money minded. She had released my brother from their sessions as soon as she could. Damini, her name. She didn't have a fancy office like every other doctor who treated patients more like customers. Can't even trust medical personnel anymore. The first time I went to her I was very happy to see that she had two sofas in her drawing room. One in which she would sit and listen and the other one in which I would sit and talk. She wouldn't throw judgements. She wouldn't try to interpret the situation. She would just listen and give me steps to follow for a better life. That's what life was about. Knowing the problem and getting solutions. Maybe that's why I was so comfortable around her. Maybe that's why I had seen a low in my anxious episodes. I was a confident person, one of my forte is public speaking. I could talk to anyone anywhere. Even if my leg would shake, I would put a hand in my pocket to hold it still. It was weird that someone like me would go throw anxious episodes. There was a time when I roamed the city of Goa in an underwear and a t-shirt because someone had stolen my jeans. That's the amount of fucks I gave to anyone's opinion. So why did Meera's opinion and actions fuck me up? Why did the one thing she said, kill my happy go lucky vibe. Maybe because she made me face the music. Maybe because I couldn't ignore my problems anymore.

Most of my sessions with Damini were about my family or Meera. There was a time when I requested her to give me some medication so that I don't feel like shit anymore. She didn't. I hated her a bit for that.

She told me repeatedly that I was a strong mature person who was doing the right things in his life. Was she re-assuring me about my actions?

You know, you would always tell a mentally weak person that they were not weak. Keep them ignorant of their own condition. Ignorance was bliss. Always will be.

There was a session in which I asked her, "What's the purpose of life? What are we doing here? Are we just passing time till the day we die? What's the importance of any of it? You are a therapist, you fix people but what is the long term goal for you? What are you getting out of it except keeping yourself busy? Have you never taken a step back to look at the bigger picture? Have you never wondered if life is worth living?"

She looked worried. She took a deep breath and started spewing what seemed to be a mix of rapping and preaching. Preaching life.

"Life is not supposed to be exceptional, Abeer. Life is supposed to be life. The only reason you should live is for life itself. Nothing else. Not for yourself. Not for your family. Not for Siddharth. Not for Meera. Life is supposed to be lived. That's one of the strong rules you should abide by."

At that point of time it sounded like standard bullshit. Now that I think about it, it was right. It was straight and to the point. Kid, don't live for other people or things. Live because there is life. No matter how it's treating you, you'll be fine. One day you'll be stronger than your troubles. Someday you'll look back and see it was all worth it. It's not wrong to love someone. It's not wrong to depend on someone. Just don't stop existing because of their absence.

In the recent session, we talked about the events of Shillong. The natural attraction and artificial repulsion between us. How sure I was about her and how sure she couldn't be. Damini suggested me that I ask Meera to decide. Firmly. That's the one thing I couldn't follow.

Meera in all her confusion seemed devastated by whatever happened in her past. I had met enough people to realise that the anxiety she had built up was because something old was triggering her. Something old, something wicked. Meera was a sweet woman who at points was a kid. She would lose her temper, get excited at things as if there was no tomorrow, she would trust people without second thought and she'd be kind to everyone without regrets. She was like I used to be before Shivangi died. I remember that now. Even when she wouldn't show it, she'd need security and love. She'd need reassurance. Her brain functioned like a mature adult who had seen life but her heart ran rampant like a teenager's. That's what I loved about her. Being kind and caring comes with a cost of being hurt repeatedly. That never stopped her. I just didn't want to hurt her. She was meant to be loved. Loved by me.

Damini told me this in my best interests with the fear of what might happen if things didn't workout. She didn't realise that love wasn't a feeling or an event. It was a promise. We were just two kids in a situation that seemed dire.

It was funny how whenever we would meet, we'd run off to places unplanned. To event unforeseen. To roads untravelled.

Damini was right, I had to take a stand. So I did. I took a stand to protect her until she hurts me herself, purposefully. I was just a human. I had let go of my ego but self respect is something I wouldn't sacrifice. I would make all the efforts for her on the cost of my time and energy but not on the cost of my being. Remember that in love. Don't let anyone treat you worse than you would treat them. Over time, I realised that to my long texts Meera had one word replies. Meera, would talk when she had the time. I would talk to her avoiding everyone else. Meera wasn't wrong here. I was. Too much of anything is harmful. A hell lot of love is as toxic as Cyanide and Happiness. So, I pulled back a bit. Stopped being all lovey dovey even when I wanted to be. Self control is a pursuit.

One fine day, I was talking to Meera lying on a bench in front of my house. (I could lie down anywhere.) I hadn't asked much of her. To think of it I hadn't asked anything of her except things she should've done for her own well being. The kisses were not a favour on me, but on the both of us. It was out of affection, not out of need. If they were a favour, it would be so much worse. If someone loves you, don't ever love them as a favour. Don't ever love them because they love you. Love them because you are happy around them, love them because of who they are and what they do for the world. Love them for their character, ambition and sex appeal. Never for their feelings. My biggest fear at this point was that Meera didn't love me, she loved the fact that I loved her so much that she didn't have to love me back.

"Abeer, I just came out of one bad thing and you're pressuring me into another thing." Meera roared.

All I asked her was if she liked me. I needed some reassurance. Was it such a bad thing? Was it a crime? I wouldn't know. It was the first time in my life I wanted someone to tell me that they like me. I was never much for words. She had her own demons. I realised that maybe after the kisses I was being clingy. Maybe I was being weird. So I decided to take a step back, look at the bigger picture. I hit the gym, got my mind cleared up and talked to her later that night. Not like I would after Shillong, but like I would talk to her before Shillong. Neither of us needed complications. I had to stop putting both of us in positions that would hurt us.

It was her decision to make a move now. I would never

assume. I would never ignore her for not loving me. She was a strong independent woman who had to make a decision.

Damini laughed at me, "Abeer, you're a twenty-two year old guy who has lost three close people to depression these past four months. Two of them who were under your care. You lost your best friends in the pursuit of love. You are the one who needs to be taken care of. You don't have to take care of everyone. You are a kid. All you have to do is, be one."

I snickered. She was right but life wasn't that simple anymore. That was like saying, "Are you depressed? Be happy, my friend."

Damini did have a point but Meera had been through enough too. Damini was just worried about me because I was her patient.

Meera needed to decide. In her own due time under her own comfort without any pressure by me.

It was back to basics. It was not about capturing her. It was about seeing her look at the stars from a window of a grey 2016 Toyota Innova, it was about dancing with her at a concert, it was about seeing her ask a random guy to teach her how to smoke, it was about hugging her in a tent, feeling safe and it was about experiencing life with her.

Damini and I, ended that session with laughter. Actual laughter after a long long time. If Damini wasn't my therapist I would love her to be my drinking buddy.

I told her that I was almost going to punch Vijay because he thought Meera was using me to fill a void. Siddharth punched his shoulder on my behalf. Who isn't filling a void? Who can blame people, they didn't know Meera like I did. All they could do was make judgements to ease their pain of understanding.

In life, listen to everyone but follow your own instincts. Even if it turns out to be a mistake, it was your own. Make your own mistakes. Also, friends have a tendency to hate your love interests anyhow. That's just their instincts kicking in.

"She is not using you. You are not using her. There is something else going on here and no one knows what it is. Not even either one of you. This is just a classic love story or a tragedy. Either ways, you'll be fine. Both of you have been through much worse. Breakups and rejections are at the bottom of the food chain here." Damini told me what I already knew.

"Let's see. We are in a movie, right? We won't know how it ends, until it ends." I replied.

I am better now. Life seems worthwhile. I laugh and sleep. Life should be lived for just because it's life. Trust me, it'll be better. It was a conclusion to a chapter. How do you maintain your sanity through a shit storm? Keep walking. You'll get out at one point. Meera kept walking too. I was proud of her for it. I am just waiting for her here with me holding some of the quality vodka she loves. My eyes waiting to see the excitement in her eyes, every time she sees vodka. She was a wild animal, she needed to follow her instincts and come home if she wanted to. Like I told her in the car last night, I was right here. I wasn't going anywhere. Therapy is not bad, just look for someone experienced and kind. Someone who you can trust.

Dear reader, in the pursuit of love, sleep apnea and depression, think about what makes you happy. I finally had the answer. It didn't lie with her, it lied within me. The only way I would be happy was if I didn't fail anyone else in my life. Love is not an event or a feeling, it's a promise.

•••

The Office Romance or Something

"When someone really, really likes you. You can smell it of them. If you observe carefully, you'll see it. Just ask yourself one thing. 'Is there something materialistic they are getting out of you?'. If the answer is No, they're into you." Siddharth told me on the terrace of Pragati Vihar Hostels when we were in 10th standard. Life was simple. I was a kid who was asocial. Siddharth was showing me the ropes to getting all the women you like. He had a way with women, like I hadn't seen. Siddharth would always woo a girl he liked. I never got the hang of it.

"Relationships are a power struggle. Don't watch bollywood movies, that's what makes you a hopeless romantic. Romance never helped anyone achieve anything," said Siddharth. I didn't believe him back then. Now, that I have had the experience of love and relationships I realised one thing. When guys love a girl with all their heart, they don't know what to do with them. They become Gamma Males. They hand them everything on a platter. I have seen guys going to the lengths of paying their crush's phone bills, doing there laundry, ignoring friends and family for them and killing time in the process. Don't fall in love with someone who doesn't love you back. Know when to get up and walk away. It wasn't time for me to walk away from Meera but Damini was right.

"Don't give up your life for someone who won't even call you when they're around family. Don't share everything with someone who doesn't share much with you."

Some people have mastered the art of sharing so less and making you believe that you know a lot about them. I knew some things about Meera. I knew who she was but, my reader, do you remember the only rule I have for people? The only thing you can know about a person is what they want to share with you.

It was time. Time to start thinking about what I was doing. Where this was going. Now, that I was out of self loathing, idolising people and helping everyone without considering my feelings I saw a clearer image.

In the history of time, there was no gamma male who got the girl. There was no person who selflessly loved a girl who he wooed later on. It is basic psychology. People don't respect anything that comes naturally to them. Love was a power struggle but I would rather be Meera's friend than play mind games with her. She was too pure for me to mess with that. I loved her too much for that. So, what I had to do was focus on myself. Try that. You'll feel great.

Last week, just on the day before Diwali I was playing my guitar at the office. With the Meera syndrome, all I could play was sad songs. I didn't even take a pill in Ibiza. I was donning my signature shades, with an unkempt beard, eye brows giving no fucks about authority and body language that disregarded life itself. That's how a girl described me when she was recording me. I didn't know her. She didn't know me. She seemed like a sweet innocent girl, I was someone who had seen enough shit to realise, "It's a trap."

I asked her to send me the recording then I parted ways. We saw each other everyday at work but after what happened to my intern I was in no mood to talk to any office girls. At least the ones that didn't initiate the conversation.

It was a week ago. Now I was sitting in my squad talking about how drugs have a thing about them. How money, sex and drugs are the answer to most questions in life. Questions like existence, depression, stress and validation. It can't answer one question, Love and Life. The only questions in the pursuit of happiness. The only answer for them is ignorance.

So this unnamed girl found ways to talk to me. Why was she pursuing me out of all people? The answer to that was lost to me. When someone shows interest in me, my first instinct is, "What do they want?" That's a genuine question worth asking. Helps you react better to the situation. This girl seemed to want my attention. No other area of interest as of now. Validation and love is something people seek too. What I was seeking from Meera. I had stopped trying fill a void with someone who created more voids. Abeer was trying to put off fires using fuel. Abeer was an ignorant fuck like most of you idiots. I still loved the hell out of Meera. Just not enough to let her dictate my life. She was not capable of loving me right now. She had her own battles to fight.

Coming to the office girl. Let's call her Mona Darling. Mona Darling was a hardworking professional. Her field of work involved video editing in abundance. She would be stuck at her desk with a ponytail working out the dynamics of cinema. I found that very interesting. Big fan of cinema, me.

Both of us were working late that fine evening. It was ten p.m. I was surviving a 10 hour shift. Mona was there before me. All of our colleagues had went home. It was just us on the first floor of a very beautiful office. She smiled at me, so did I. She came to talk to me. She told me that I play beautifully and maybe her firm would need some composer in the future. So now I knew what she was in for. I told her that I am no composer, I just play sad rock music. She seemed disappointed. I wasn't. I asked her about her work. She seemed very enthusiastic about it. She worked for an advertisement firm in post processing. It was good to see someone in love with what they did. Enthusiastic people are usually a pain in the ass. They expect everyone around them to be as excited and happy. That wasn't the case with Meera or Mona Darling. They didn't demand happiness, they radiated it.

Missing Meera was easy. Loving her was hard. Not loving her was way harder. Meera had taken multiple tests to see whether I was worth her time, it was time for me to be sure too. No matter how great she was, I had to see if she was right for me. So, I tried to do that in my best capacity.

Meanwhile, Mona Darling and I decided to go to the metro

station together. I would've been fine without her around too. All I needed was a book and some music. While talking to her, I realised she had a lot of habits similar to Meera's. Emotional trauma was pretty visible in her too.

I think I realised one thing then, she was looking for the same thing. Validation and support. I didn't have any for her.

Meera and I, in our Naivety didn't realise that we were. She would kiss me back and ask me to forget about it. She would fight about basic things and ask me to forget about it. There are just some things that are embedded in your memory. My mood would go totally off when I saw the hotel in which Meera's friends got beaten up by bouncers. My mood goes off when I would beautiful songs I shared with her is played. That's just the expense of loving someone who doesn't love you. You fuck your life up piece by piece. I needed to know what she wanted with me. If you ever love someone, don't ever ask them to move on just because you are scared. If you need time, ask them to wait. There are no rules in love.

So, for the same reason I couldn't afford to look at Mona the same way. She was just someone I was talking to. This is a vicious circle, people loving wrong people and in the process ignoring the potentially right ones. Everyone realised this but no one could do anything about it. She was cute, yes. I couldn't shake off thinking of Meera whenever Mona would do something sweet. I even called her Meera twice. It was very late and Mona had a place nearby. She asked me if I wanted to stay over. I declined. I didn't need more drama in this one life. It was like I was breaking on the inside and I was pretending to be happy on the outside. Even fooling myself in that process.

Mona seemed disappointed again. So was I. She was a great girl. I was just in love with a stupid one. Either Meera didn't care about me or she didn't realise the impact of her actions. Maybe she was just the classic girl people warn each other about. The Succubus. Maybe she was a kid who had nothing to offer to anyone, anymore. With her justified trust issues and my inability to mistrust, we were lost. There were plenty of fish in the sea but we were just two lost souls swimming in a fish bowl.

Just one thought stuck in my head on the highway back to Delhi. That's just the lover's curse. That's just the vicious circle. Funnily enough, I still don't know her name.

•••

Questions

Do you want something? Do you need it? Do you live for wants or do you live for needs? Do you use the latest iPhone or are you satisfied with a lowly android? Do objects bring you happiness? Are you materialistic? Are you religious or spiritual? Are you rich enough to have enough happiness to overshadow the sorrow? Do you need dark rum or do you need a glass of long island iced tea? Have you ever had a smoke without a reason? Have you loved someone enough to let them go? Have you kissed someone and forgotten your issues? Do you love yourself? Would you date yourself if you were in the position of your love interest? When you say goodbye, do you kiss their forehead or their lips? Do you need love to refuel your lost soul? Are you counting on someone else to heal you? Is there a moment or place in your life that you would want to stay in forever? Do you live in the past, present or the future?

I bet like you, Meera and I, also had different answers to each one of these questions. Even life long spouses would have conflict of interest here. Just because the answer would be different doesn't mean that there is no love here. Meera and I, had a lot of things we needed to sort. She would never take the initiative because I wasn't that important to her. She didn't love me. I was just an object that brought her temporary happiness. Like a kid who has ice-cream to mend their broken heart. They can't have ice cream forever right? They have to grow up. Meera was either rebounding and I was there or she loved the fact that I love her. In the words of the great Siddharth Sinha, "If someone loves you, you can smell it off them. There is always a smell of roses and diarrhoea at the same time."

Okay, direct question : Did I want to fuck, Meera? I don't think so. Maybe I do but it is not my primary concern. She is hot but not hot enough to make me materialistic about love suddenly. No one broke my heart more than I did by overthinking everything. So, there was a series of questions I needed answers to. The questions I forgot when I saw her. The questions that broke me even by her slightest sign of indifference. So, I read some research papers to figure out why Meera had an anxiety attack after kissing me. It's pretty common, even for couples that have been married for a long time. Women live a traumatised life. Everywhere they go. The subway, concerts, clubs, footpaths and even within the safe walls of their homes. In Indian society, sex for women has been represented as something that is done to them. No one tells them that they can enjoy it too. They are taught to protect their "fragile" bodies from the vicious claws of every male. It's not entirely false either. People do use each other for sex. It's hard to recognise the intentions of Men around them. And after what Meera had been through, much harder. One can only be fooled so many times.

I had a strong feeling that Meera's anxiety attack was a result of one of the two things:

1. Someone had been insensitive to her sexual comfort in the past.
2. She became vulnerable and she thought I would leave her too. She couldn't go through that again.

I could be easily wrong. It's not her fault if she was abused. It's not her fault if she was cheated on. It's not her fault if she was manipulated. It's not her fault if she was taken advantage of. At this point of time, my meeting with Meera was not about our love life. It was about her past.

She was scared. I could smell it off her that night. All I did was hug her and reassure her that I was right here. I wasn't going anywhere. What made me really sad was that she apologised to me for being uncomfortable.

I told her, "Don't be sorry for that Meera. I am sorry." Imagine, someone's first response to being uncomfortable in a loving moment was to apologise to the other individual. Kid, you don't need to apologise to anyone for being uncomfortable for anything. She didn't owe me anything.

Naturally, if you thought of it like I do, you'd be as worried as I was. I am sitting in a bar waiting for her to come so that I can talk it out with her. I had to make some notes on my mobile phone so that I didn't forget anything. It went like this:

Anxiety:

1. Abused in the past
2. Kissing me reminds her of someone else
3. Supressing emotions. Sudden outburst in a moment of vulnerability.

The Book:

Why couldn't you read it?

Me:

What do you think of me? Are there any insecurities? Worried that I'll leave too?

With that I was prepared to ask her all the questions I needed. I vomited twice because I am very anxious of the answers I will get. I am also worried if she would go for the defence mechanism and lash out like she did every time we got serious.

There is a scene in my favourite movie, Tamasha. In that movie, the protagonist, Ved, was mentally disturbed because the love of his life, Tara, made him face the hard truth. He lashes out at her. He goes into defence mechanism. The lights and theme of this bar is the same one from the movie. It is most probably the same bar too. Tara asks Ved to meet him at a bar so that they can talk and she can mellow his pain down. Ved shows reluctance but ultimately shows up. In that scene, they start out by being the friendliest they could be. At one point of time, Tara accidentally triggers another insecurity in Ved. She makes the look on his face, change. She then chooses her next words very carefully, she was scared. It was too late. Ved rushed into defence mechanism again. Tara begged him to stay, he didn't. He couldn't. That's what love is. Insecurities, care, desperation, attraction and repulsion.

Meera called.

"Abeer, I am near the bar. Do I come in?"

"No. I'll come downstairs." The bar was crowded and I wouldn't have been able to talk to her properly. Also, we would probably end up getting drunk and making out again and I wouldn't want that until she knew what she wanted.

I went out of the bar. I immediately spotted her. It wasn't hard for me to spot her anywhere. You know how you look at some people and you don't see the crowd around them? I walked up to her. She was as beautiful as a cold winter evening. It was unreal. Over time I had seen one thing change. Meera's eyes seemed way brighter when she looked at me. Her voice had grown softer naturally around me. She came in for a hug. It felt amazing. As usual. I had to pull back. There were some points I had to discuss.

•••

A Broken Dining Table

It's been a long time since I've written anything. May be, because I have been happier. Happiness is the death of art. That's true for me, at least. I never create art when I am happy. Sorrow fuels me in a way. Today the reason for my unhappiness is not Meera, no. I will take you to the basics of my dysfunction today. What shaped me into who I am, Family.

Let me fill you in what's happening with Meera, first. Let's get it out of the way so we can focus on the fucked up extravaganza that is everyone's family. After our conversation about my list, Meera and I had established that we like each other.

"Why do you get serious anxiety when you're vulnerable around me, Meera?"

"I… I have thought about it." It was difficult for her to maintain eye contact but then her eyes turned to me. They were strong. "What I could think of was the fact that maybe subconsciously… maybe subconsciously I have developed a fear that you will leave too. That this won't last."

Somehow, my reader, I knew that was the thing. I told her I was not going anywhere. I was right there. That I love her. She had serious commitment issues that was justified. We established that whatever this is, it's mutually exclusive. That's all I wanted to know. We then went on as full on couples do. No restraint, no second thoughts. We knew we were fond of each other and we weren't really considerate what anyone else thought about it. Long story short, we are together. We are just not calling it that. Meera, dropped me home that night. Hugged me tight and at the end, just gave me a small kiss on my nose. I didn't know how to respond to that.

Meera, now, was a solid asset for me. She was my muse. What (probably) seemed was to be the love of my life. There are three kind of people in your life who are important aspects of it.

1. Those you love, adore and care about.
2. Those you are indifferent about.
3. Those you hate thoroughly and you don't know why.

There was not any I can think of that I'd hate. I mean, I do hate Meera sometimes on account of how far she was. I would see her each day everyday but that wasn't possible. We had our families, our work, our passions and our friends. Other aspects of our life. It was all going to be turned upside down wanting me to see her more.

Let's see.

At work an intern killed himself, client were wanting to leave left and right, there was intense gender based politics at our co-working space and I hated every moment I had to talk to some dumb fuck with undue respect because they were a client. Meera would understand that. The next time you're on a flight notice how some special people are particularly respectful to the hospitality team.

My friends were doing great. They always have been. No matter how our lives would be fucked up we would always stay together and make ourselves happier version of our very fucked up selves.

My family is another story we'll talk about.

To sum it up, there was nowhere I could turn at that point except her. I hate being needy so I took a step back. Sure, it was a time of need but a person's character is defined by how he deals with a crisis.

It was the day after Meera and I cleared what we were doing here. What was happening. There was not much happening at the office so I sent people home and left the office myself. I went to see Siddharth. I told him what happened and he was all smiley and happy. Don't you love it when your friends are happy for you? We had a few drinks and a fun time. It was time for me to go home. I hated going home these days. I reached home buzzing. Hard to keep a straight face. My parents were going out for dinner. I had the house to myself.

Somehow, I didn't want to stay in that night. I called Meera and I told her that I wanted to meet up. It was 10 p.m. We decided to meet near her place. We went out for some coffee. I told her about the whole scenario of fucked up random shit that was being thrown at the wall. Like I told you, she didn't demand happiness. She radiated it. That's maturity and kindness. Next thing we know, we are walking around in her colony. A cold winter night, some liquor buzz and your lover by your side. What dreams are made of. That night had everything I loved. Her hand in mine. Some cold black coffee. Long pointless walks.

There was a time when we built a moment. A moment that promised great face battles. Late night, in the middle of the street. There was a bike next to us. Neither of us realised there was someone standing by it. As soon as he started his bike our eyes turned to him.

"Hi, bhai." I said. She started laughing.

"Hi." The dude was dazed and confused.

He pulled his bike out, and he was going to leave.

"Bye, bhai." He said.

"Bye." I replied. Meera couldn't stop laughing. Yes I know. We're cute and weird. Mostly weird, but cute too.

Admirable, how men turn out to be the best and cooperative beings as soon as they see some other man in a compromising place. They always have each other's back. It's something that is programmed in every decent man's mind. It's called "The Universal Bro Code."

In the pursuit of some privacy, we ended up in a small alley. I was worried she'd be hit by her anxiety again.

So, I kept asking her again and again if she was okay. I knew that she'd have trouble stopping even if she wants to and I didn't want to see her with that exhausted face again. The alley was dark and there was a tree above us through which bright white street light was falling on us. There was also a moment when she went silent and was disturbed. I knew it might've been because I overdid it somewhere. Her head was on my shoulder. My head was on her left shoulder. The back of her neck in my hand, I was gently massaging it. There was nothing about this woman that I didn't love.

There was nothing I had to put up with. It was all my pleasure. She was a being that didn't belong to this tainted world and I was lucky that she chose to look in my direction for all this period of time. I rubbed her back with my other hand, reassuring her that I was here. I wasn't going anywhere.

"Abeer, I don't want to be close right now." The first thing she said in the past few minutes.

I took a step back. We stood in that alley facing each other while there was light on her and just her. She was looking down. It was hard to make eye contact for her. Whenever she had even the slightest of anxieties, her face would change.

Her cheeks would get puffed. Her mouth would be open like it was about to ask "why?"

Not "Why did you kiss me, Abeer?"

It would be more like, "Why is this happening, Abeer? Why does it feel good and bad at the same time?"

I wasn't sure what it was.

It was heartbreaking looking at her. She looked up.

"You should move on, Abeer."

"Why?"

"I don't think you'll be happy here. I don't thing I am ready."

"I am my happiest here. If you're ready ask me to wait, don't ask me to go away. You just have to ask."

Her short hair were covering half her face. The other half was the face my nightmares and daydreams were made of.

"It hurts how beautiful you are." I felt like shit thinking she looked beautiful when she was down.

That's all I could say. Her eyes were locked with mine and I was not sure but what something felt off. The expression on my face felt very different, very wrong. It was the small things she did that made a whole lot of difference to me. How she would give me peck on my nose sometimes. How she'd touch my hair sometimes. How she'd have the tightest hugs for me every now and then. It was weird how in the pursuit of me trying to help her, she was helping me. That's why I was confused maybe. So, I just hugged her. We were fine. We were growing.

Things weren't as bad as they could've been. It's just funny you don't realise how much you crave love and affection until someone comes your way and shows you, what you didn't have. What you've always needed.

I never knew how much I needed someone to run their hands through my hair with thorough affection, I never knew how I needed someone to give me a weird peck on my nose every now and then, I never knew I needed someone to hold my hand as I walked in the cold winter nights. I never realised I needed someone to hint that I needed to quit smoking, not because they thought it was gross but because they cared about me. This my friends is called the Man-Puppy Syndrome.

At every point in your life, you could associate your feelings with a beautiful dog breed to gain a broader idea of what you craved. No matter what dog breed you deal with. No matter how scary they may seem. No matter how sad or angry they are, if you hit them the right way you'll realise all they needed was love and affection. It's the same way with you. No matter what you've seen, no matter how hard life's been and no matter how much damage you've done, genuine care and affection heals you.

That night in the alley, I didn't know the answers to Meera's problems. It was weird for a know all to not know what to do with something so crucial. She was hurt. She was left. She didn't deserve it. Not because she was beautiful (which she is) but because she is a kind human being who helps people at her own cost.

Someone wise once told me, "If someone is trying to help even when they have their own shit to figure out, that's love."

Siddharth and Meera, were those people for me. My father sacrificed a lot for me too. I bet there is a lot that I don't appreciate when it comes to my family. I feel ungrateful at points. Maybe, I am It was just hard to love people who you constantly saw fighting each other over insecurities, envy and clinginess. There were mornings when I'd wake up to screaming and fighting. It was mostly when my grandfather was around. One tends to notice these small details when they've worked as an analyst for sometime. Whenever someone from my father's side was around in the family, a major fight would be due. My father is a good person, he helps everyone he can. There is something conventionally wrong with genuine people, they can be too trusting.

My father had his own financial and social struggles while growing up. There was never a materialistic thing he'd not let me have if it was in his financial capacity. I am what you would call, a spoiled brat. My elder brother and father always protected me and gave me everything I needed even if it was the expense of their own happiness. There were times my dad would buy me a playstation at the cost of a watch he'd always wanted. He bought me laptops and took my older ones saying, "Ohh. I just need to work on powerpoint and excel. Maybe, browse the internet a little." Maybe, that's why it was difficult for me to see him disappointed. Maybe that's why I sacrificed a lot of my social life in these past five months just to keep him happy.

Ever since, Meera entered my life a lot of my time went on her and my own struggles. All this while, I took a break from my family because I didn't want to add to their issues. They didn't mind. They had their own social life which was a blessing.

This fine afternoon I am laying on the floor of my living room. My dad is sitting on the sofa. My grandfather is sitting at the dining table.

All of us are doing nothing but staring at the ceiling. This is what life is now. I am sitting here wondering it all went so wrong. Where did we push each other away so easily? It wouldn't be sad if we never talked properly. We did. We'd have been together and tell each other everything. I had my reasons to stay away from them. Let's just say, I can't tell you these reasons. My grandfather would whisper things in my Dad's ears and he'd be naive enough to believe them against his own instincts. That teaches you a lesson, my reader, don't try to please people. I would never hurt Meera or Siddharth for the sake of my family's happiness, or vice versa. My father even after being a giver all his life, someone who people look up to and respect, struggled to have my attention. He had my respect and obedience, but even after trying a lot he couldn't have a conversation with me. Whenever we talk, it'd be about work, studies, my short-comings or some random bollywood movie. That's the thing with fathers in India, in their pursuit and struggle of providing for the family they don't think of interacting with them.

There was a morning when I told my mother that I wanted to move out.

She asked me what any parent would. "Why?"

I replied, "Because I don't want to wake up hearing screams every day."

She implied that it was because of the new found love in my life, that I needed more privacy and I was using excuses. I calmly denied her stake in this.

The discussion suddenly turned into an argument. It was a long time since I had been actually angry. We didn't drive another person crazy in the house, right?

The vicious circle was starting. My parents were doing to me what their parents did to them. That's what life was now. It escalated to the length where I had to punch through the dining table to shut everyone up. I loved doing it too. Aggression can be really helpful sometimes.

That shut everyone up. My mother turned to me. She asked me to stay because she needed me. That life would've been too haywire around the other men in the house. How could I say no? Some sacrifices should be made by children too.

When Meera told me about the memories she had with her father, I could not relate. I could only be happy for her. When I think about memories with my parents, memories that were out of routine and independent of special occasions the memories would be my dad teaching me for my JEE mains, my mom texting on random whatsapp groups while her son is sitting right next to her trying to communicate.

My brother and I still shared a better bond. We shared things out of wants. We'd go have milkshakes when I was down. We'd drink beer and smoke cigarettes. We would play video games and watch movies. Now that I think about it, that's what a family is. Siddharth was family too. The times we had. The silent cold rooftops, the drinking games, the morning Chole Bhature, the late winter night ice-creams and the talks we had after our respective breakups.

Now, I was forming new memories with Meera. Memories that were so beautiful that even our break up or her marriage wouldn't taint them. Memories that could make batman smile.

It's funny how now what Meera and I had was somewhere between "adoration and sexual tension." It was pure warmth in my chest whenever I thought about her or her piggy nose.

Meera had become an escape from what this life was. The familiar fights. The vicious circle. The office politics. The hatred or indifference my family had developed in it's belly. The death all around me. Meera, was helping me grow and learn. She was helping me see the same fucked up world in a very positive manner. Everything else was already down the gutter, I just didn't want either of us to be down there too.

•••

The Beautiful

Let me tell you a story. A story of a girl that I knew. A girl who went through similar circumstances as Shivangi. While travelling through Egypt, I developed a strong bond with one of the local representatives of the country. Hazem. Life was simpler then. We would get drunk, we would smoke all the time. Cigarettes were unexplored territory for me back then. It's funny that I only started smoking when I wanted to and not when most people were doing it around me. One of my qualities out of the many flaws is that I am not swayed by peer pressure. I like to make my own mistakes.

There was a night in Egypt when Hazem and I went out drinking. Hazem wanted to show me a place in Alexandria. He told me to put my best clothes on and meet me downstairs in 30 minutes. It was great how he would always take me places I would like to go to. He would know what was on my mind. After a night of light drinking, intense dancing and cringy singing we decided to head back home. It was 3:00 a.m. We reached our apartment and realised that the key was nowhere to be found. Luckily, our third flat mate had made a genius decision to sleep in that night. We rang the bell, knocked the door and called his number repeatedly and received no response. It made sense since we came back from a two day trek the previous morning. He was tired enough to be dead asleep. Lucky bastard. Hazem and I looked at each other and started laughing. There was a girl who used to live in the apartment opposite to mine. She had a creepy vibe to her and I used to watch a lot of horror movies back then. So I tried to avoid her as much as I could. Hazem, had gone to look for the guard and see if he had a master key. The girl approached me and initiated a conversation.

"Locked out, huh?"

"Yeah. Sleepy flat-mate…" I was a bit creeped out.

She had big beautiful eyes, messy hair and a rose ring that could fit on my thumb. I am a big guy.

"You aren't from around here, are you?"

"No, I am from India."

"Ohhh!!! The land of Taj Mahal and Shah Rukh Khan!!"

I laugh about it now but whenever someone in Egypt got to know that I was from India this would be their first reaction. People would either talk about Taj Mahal, Shah Rukh Khan, Amitabh Bacchan or Aamir Khan. It is funny now because if it comes to the current government, Taj Mahal would be called Ram Mandir. Sometimes, people in Egypt would come to me and start talking to me in Arabic and I would reply in Hindi. According to them, I looked like an Egyptian and according to me most Egyptians looked pretty Indian.

"Do you want to come in and have a coffee?" She asked.

"Sure." I was a bit dazed and confused. To my surprise she was making Turkish coffee. I loved it. I miss it.

"So, what brings you to Egypt?"

"Actually, there was an opportunity and free time. Student exchange is the way to be."

"Ohhh, so you are in a college. How old are you?"

"I just turned nineteen."

"Ohhhhh so you are a kid. I am twenty-three."

"Good for you." I was cocky.

"Tell me something about yourself."

"Well, I am an Indian B.Tech student. I have a great family, my friends are pretty cool and I don't know what I want to be in the future but I have interest in photography."

"Ohhh, photography? Do you work on photoshop a lot? I am a digital artist."

"I don't know much about digital art. I am pretty ignorant that way."

"Let me show you."

Let's call her Rumi. Rumi went on to show me paintings she had made for herself and advertising material she had made for clients. Somehow her own work seemed like art as fine as Jesus would make out of water and her professional work seemed like something she had to shit out for someone else's pleasure. Isn't that what being a professional artist is mostly? Being a genius who works at the whim of sheeple?

There was a painting I remember distinctly. There was a girl sitting in a room as small as a dispensary in Palampur, she was sitting expressionless with light falling on her in strips as they passed from what presumably was a window blind and she had this expression in her eye much like the one Meera had in hers in the alley. That same haunting sight.

That brought up the same question in my mind. The question that draws me to people the most.

"What was the worst thing you've been through?"

"What? Is that what you ask someone the first time you meet them?"

"Not really. This is the first time this question came to my mind."

She opened her mouth to say something but then my phone rang. It was Hazem. He was in the corridor looking for me and I told him I was inside the other girl's apartment. Room 503. Hazem came in too. It was a bit awkward since the conversation we were having had shifted it's dynamic from dark and brooding to something out of a sitcom. Rumi and I would glance at each other even when Hazem was talking because we knew there was something urgent here. Something that needed addressing. Once Hazem went to sleep, which was around 6:00 a.m., she made me another cup of coffee and she told something. She told me that she couldn't sleep usually. She couldn't sleep at all. She was happy that she wasn't alone tonight as she didn't like being alone at nights. This was the first time I had met someone suffering from insomnia. People threw around that word casually like it was something cool. She told me most of the work that I liked was painted at nights. A lot of them were nude images of people who seemed distressed to say the least.

Only one of them was a peaceful image of a woman wearing a Hijab. Rumi told me that it was her mother. Rumi used to live in Syria and she had to flee to Egypt because of the war. The unwanted war. She was separated from her family when she was seventeen and didn't have anywhere to go in Egypt. So, she seeked asylum at her uncle's place. Her uncle's family provided for her, gave her shelter but at the same time she was subjected to abuse like anything I had heard before. The details are not mine to share. The details are hurtful, my reader. At the same time, they would make you grateful for what you have and weep for someone you don't even know. This is not my story to tell. I didn't hug her or touch her because it was physically awkward. Also, Egypt is a "tad" conservative.

7:00 a.m. Rumi wanted to go for a walk. There was a beach nearby. Alexandria has beautiful beaches and buildings. We walked to the beach. Alexandria, has one of the most beautiful skies I've ever seen. You don't see sights like that in a place called Delhi. I love India. To love is to accept something with its flaws clear to you. We lay on the cold sand of the December beach. I remember looking at her and how she seemed so happy and sad at the same time. Some people who laugh a lot just need a push to fall into despair. I didn't want to test that limit. We looked up on a grateful sky, felt wise waves of wind on our faces and restlessness in our heart. Maybe it was all the caffeine. Maybe it was the tragedy. Maybe it was both.

Rumi and I, exchanged numbers. Promised we would stay in touch. Hazem stayed in touch with her, too. The following year Hazem and Rumi, started seeing each other and they got married in 2017. I was invited but couldn't go because of how fuck-all private colleges are. We still facetime sometimes. Life feels good when I think of them.

Her story was much like Shivangi's. She was deserted. Put through abuse from familiar places. The difference being one of them held on long enough to see a better day and the other one couldn't. No one is better or worse here but it just makes you think, will life be better if you just show some courage and patience? I really believe, so. An year ago, I was contemplating suicide, sleeping for 18 hours straight, avoiding people and drinking every time I'd get. Now, I have a decent job, my friends, my family and Meera's hand in mine. Now, I just need decent amount of coffee in the morning and I am somewhat of a happier entity. Life doesn't necessarily feed off on your misery, sometimes it rewards you for your patience.

•••

The Solo Trip

Have you ever been on a solo trip? What a wonderful experience it is. You meet new people who broaden your horizons, you see places as per your own comfort and interest and most importantly there is no one to hold you back. You don't have to think about the interests and disinterests of your fellow travellers. Friendships make and break on solo trips. Why do friendships mostly break when you come back from a solo trip? Mostly it's because you're a different person while you're travelling. You have a general curiosity for things. You love what you are doing because you're doing it for yourself. In this state of Euphoria, when you meet someone they will most probably have a very positive experience around you and vice versa. This obviously develops a certain sense of comfort and affection between people which then results in "Friendships." We call them friends but we don't know what they are like at their worst. We just know what they feel like at their best. That's why friendships break after a solo trip. You go back to your usual life, your "holiday high" is maintained for a few days. Everything seems beautiful for a maximum of approximately two weeks. What happens then is you start adjusting back to your usual life. You develop the same old fears. You deal with the same people in the same job. Your lifestyle becomes so busy that you don't have time to contact the people you once thought would be your best friends. Don't get me wrong, the fondness remains. The love remains. It is directed to the people we met on a trip, not the people they really are. Very rarely, a group of people maintain the same affection to each other, a couple of months after a trip. Why am I telling you this? So that you realise that this isn't a bad thing. You just evolved after travelling solo. You gained a certain confidence. You developed a certain love for all things and most importantly you learn that you don't necessarily need someone to enjoy your life.

Pushkar. It is known for a lot of things. There is an annual festival in Pushkar. Pushkar has the only temple in the world in which religious people pray to Lord Brahma. I remember it had something to do with Brahma being sexually attracted to his own daughter, Srishti. Makes sense, right? Meera had planned a trip to Pushkar since she got a few days off. I would do that too a couple of years back. Meera had the enthusiasm I did in first and second year of college. Have you ever met someone who was sunshine in human form?

Here is another chain of events for you. The night before she left for Pushkar, Meera and I met. Near her home again. We walked. By now you must realise, walking in winter nights is my favourite thing to do. I smoked a cigarette. She had this affection in her eyes that was pretty calming. We went to a coffee shop. We sat. Checked our respective menus, reached the conclusion there wasn't anything worth ordering. Meera was on a phone for what seemed to be fifteen minutes. I knew for a fact it was a family member on the phone. I stepped out of the coffee shop as crowded coffee shops suck as much as empty concerts. She came out in a while. We were at a point when everything was understood and the basic trust had been formed. I would constantly tell her that I loved her and I didn't know how or why. She would constantly look at me with those trusting eyes of hers and make small gestures that would mean a hell of a lot to me. I wasn't used to physical affection. She would hug me out of the blue. She would give me a small kiss on the nose. She would hug me as tight as she possibly could. It's a difficult job considering my shoulder size. The classic romantic affair. There was nothing stopping us anymore. Everything made sense. We went for a drive to look for ATMs so that she could activate her debit card. We failed miserably. We went to the mall again to get some pizza. I never had anything for pizza but she seemed enthusiastic about it. Honestly, I would eat anything thrown at me with the same excitement. The only exception being Mughalai cuisine. I fucking love it. Biryani, Korma, Sheer Mal, Khamiri Roti, Jahangiri Chicken, etc. Mouth watering, huh? After we went back to the terrace of the shopping complex.

She looked at me without the slightest doubt in her eyes and asked me rhetorically, "How and where did I meet you, Abeer?"

"In an Indigo flight. 6E 336." I replied.

Of course, I remembered the flight number. To me it was probably the only significant flight in the history of time except the ones that rammed into the World Trade Centre. It was one a.m. I had to drop Meera to the railway station the next morning at six a.m. We would have to leave by 5:30 a.m. She had to go home and pack. I had to go home and work on a presentation.

We sat in my car for a while. She held my hand and told me, "I wish you didn't have to go home tonight."

Cons of living with your family. You can't cuddle up and sleep with your significant other as much as you'd like to. I was happy she told me this honestly. For the first time it felt like she wasn't afraid of something romantic. That she wasn't second guessing herself. That she needed me a bit too. I went home a happy person that night. I reached home and finished my presentation.

It was 2:40 a.m. I had to sleep since I had to wake up at 5:15 a.m. So, I slept. There were three alarms. 4:45, 5:00 and 5:15. I woke up and talked to her. She was going to pick me up since my home was en route the railway station from her place. We reached a couple of minutes before the departure of the train. We hugged. Kissed each other on the cheeks. It was evident I wanted to go on that trip too but that's part of being a working adult. There are some trips you have to let go. She sat in the train. I waited for the train to leave. 6:15 a.m. The horn blew, the rails started. We looked at each other. I gestured, "get off." It was obviously a kid in love. I wasn't that serious too. She replied, "Get in". I swear to the soul of Freddie fucking Mercury I would jump in that train if I didn't have office. Nothing else was holding me to Delhi. Family life was going mental, friends had their own life to figure out and one can only smoke so many cigarettes. Meera felt like home too. She was peaceful. Looking at her would calm my mind more than smoking joints of Marijuana would. Kissing her would get me more excited than snorting two lines of coke would. Well, I am just assuming. Who knows why drugs are so popular? Maybe for the same reason they are obsessed with sex, they want to feel something more than they already do. I don't regret anything about it. I knew Meera was mine and there would be more trips, there would be more alcohol, more unwanted drama and a lot of wholesome moments. There was one thing that I couldn't deny. We were two people who knew exactly what the other one needed and how to make them a happier entity. Everything we had been through. Every drama, every disappointment led us to each other.

Every life experience we had made us the people who were just right for each other. Somewhat damaged, somewhat strong, somewhat reckless and extremely adorable. To one another at least.

I picked up my mother after I saw her off. We went home and I slept for an hour. It was time for me to visit a client and give them a monthly review presentation. I hated client visits for one single reason. We had to pretend to respect people who rarely deserve it. Everyone deserves respect but I wasn't sure if they deserved my professional respect. That day was hell. Working on four hours of sleep for people I despised but I was satisfied as dropping Meera off to the railway station helped her on her first solo trip. I had decided one thing and one thing only, I won't bother Meera on her trip. Let her enjoy as much as she could. My stuff could wait. It was easy as I am naturally not clingy. I love attention but I don't demand it.

On the two days of her trip, Meera would send me a few pictures of the places she had visited. The people she had met. Give me a very brief idea of the adventures she was having. I loved how excited she was about everything. I had to pretend a lot during that period because I didn't want her to know what was going on at my place. That would worry her. I am not gonna let you know either. Why? Sharing ugly details of my family would lead you to believe my family wasn't a happy place. It was. It's just that there are some phases of unhappiness in every family. Here it was an occasional shit storm.

She sent me a message that brightened up my mood instantly.

"You are missed." I loved that woman so fucking much I would kill for her.

Hell yeah. I should be missed. I deserve major missing. Jokes apart. Meera would do the smallest things and make me the happiest and I had to push my boundaries every time I wanted to make her happy. It wasn't difficult. It was the need of the hour. She deserved that. I loved her enough not to tally what we did for each other. I realise the courage she has to muster up to love me at this point in her life. She had very limited trust and she chose to put it on me. Lucky Bastard, Abeer.

The very next morning I volunteered to pick Meera up from the railway station and have breakfast with her. After that I would go home, change and go to office. She would spend time with her very loving family. Dids and Jiju, dearest. Beautiful people from what I had heard. The kid at her place had one of those voices that could make you melt out of the sheer cuteness of it. My family was difficult. Maybe I was as difficult.

The previous night, luckily I was getting sleepy. So, I called Meera to see if she left for the railway station. She cut the call. At the same time, the screaming in my house had started. I was getting anxious because of both of these events. I was worried about her so I asked her to text me. She called after a while. She was fine. She was having fun. I was relieved. At the same time, the screaming had gotten worse so I stepped out. After a while, when I cut the call I couldn't take it and I interfered. I am stupid like that. Now, I was a part of the screaming. It got so exhausting and heart breaking that I did what I always do during a fight. I walked off. I walked out of my house in boxers and slippers because the cold nights are better than fiery arguments. I had picked up a shawl.

There was a bench in front of the block. I sat on that bench and sat there for a couple of hours. Meera had slept in her train by then. The main reason I couldn't tell her anything was because

I was afraid she'd see me in a very different light because of all this. I realise that now. I went back home at 4 a.m. and I slept. I woke up at 6:30 a.m. and called Meera. She didn't pick up. Her train was supposed to arrive by seven a.m. I checked the running status of her train and it was late by an hour and half. I thought I could sleep a bit more. When I woke up Meera was already at the railway station. She was taking a cab home. She was pissed. Made sense. I had bailed on her. Not very mature of Abeer, right? She just told me that I could've told her that I wasn't able to come. She made sense. Nothing else was making sense. After a stormy night, things were calm at home. I didn't tell her what had happened because I didn't want to. She was angry. It would be better if she cooled off first.

I texted her the reason. The series of events that had led to this. To my surprise, she had no response to anything. Empathy was one of Meera's stronger traits but maybe it was on standby. I didn't want her to apologise, I didn't want her forgiveness. I just wanted her to know why. I thought I would get a free pass since I had never faltered from my commitments before. That didn't make a difference. Neither did my familiar struggles. It was almost funny. It was almost sad. That is how it is. We were falling in a vat of redundancy. I didn't want that. Whenever you think life is good, it's going great, another Salman Khan movie comes out.

Blaming her was the worst thing I could do to her and to me. Both of us deserved better. Everything we had been through got us where we wanted to be with each other. Something so small shouldn't hurt our chances at life.

•••

The Nihilist

"You know the real reason why you don't enjoy anything is because you don't believe anything. You never loved anything enough to fight for it. You can say anything against something you seem to believe. I have seen that happen around you multiple times. It's almost as if you don't love life," said Kartik.

"I do love life. I just believe it can be more than this." I replied deliberating. Was he right? When I think about it there were not a lot of things that held really value for me. It was just the people around me. The rest of the world. The material, the sense of achievement was all just pointless to me.

It had been a while since Kartik and I, talked our hearts out. It was my brother's 25th birthday. It was a huge event since my brother was going abroad in less than a month for higher education. My father suggested that I invite Kartik. Somehow my father always had more respect for people who studied than the people who were in the arts. Maybe that's the kind of person he just is. Somehow everything about my brother and I felt wrong and somehow anyone who studies. No matter, their character is made of gold. The night was fun. A lot of dancing, relationship advice to my cousins and pints of beer led my brother and I to a better place emotionally. Now, he was just spending time with my parents. Kartik and I had met after six months and a conversation was overdue. We had discussed how things went to shit because of my behaviour around Devika. I apologised. Almost teared up a bit. Then I just told him that nothing felt like anything anymore.

Everything just felt like shit. Even shit didn't feel like anything anymore.

Here is an update on my life, my reader, I have crazy happy episodes around people and as soon as I am alone I can't enjoy anything in particular. That's why I write. This gives me momentary happiness. Getting back to what Kartik had said, he was a 99% right. I could say anything against anyone in front of anyone because I didn't believe in anything. Why would I? He was slightly wrong too this time. There was someone I believed in, now. Someone whose actions made me extremely happy and extremely upset at the same time. Art didn't feel like art anymore, photography was just something every other idiot with enough money to buy a DSLR was pursuing and most importantly, who isn't an engineer or a business analyst. My Job was making me miserable. I was an unrelenting, unapologetic force of nature with the people and tasks around me before I started working. While working I was another person who used to agree to what his manager told him. I hated myself there. Maybe, that's why I had someone specific I believed in. Someone, around whom I was at my prime. I would talk to the trees and they'd talk back, I would not sleep and yet be the most energetic and I would not drink and yet be in a constant euphoria. Around that person I was not who I had become. Around that person I was who I was. She had every bit of affection in her eyes for that.

Kartik was a genius. He knew what was on my mind everytime we talked. He made a lot of sense. Siddharth and him were still my closest friends. My almost brothers. Kartik and I were tipsy.

We had subpar satisfaction that at least we don't hate each other. We are just here like it used to be in the good old days. Kartik, suggested me that I should quit my job. So did my senior at work. He asked me a simple question.

"Do you like working here?" Asked Raghav.

"Sure." I replied.

"When you came in here and I met you, you used to be someone I would not tangle within a battle of wits. I would always be afraid that you would take me down with your wits. Now I just look at you and I see that you're mostly down. That either you're scared or that you're unhappy. I am just worried about you."

I trusted him. Why? There was a time at my job that I really needed mentorship and no one stood up. Not even my own managers.

Raghav had my back. It wasn't his job to have my back. He just saw that someone was struggling and he held out his hand to help me out. That's why I trust him.

That made me question a lot of things. So, now I realised that I needed help. My own help. I needed to prioritize and perform.

Why did I not believe in anything? What are the most important aspects of a person's life? Career, family, friends and love-life. My Career was going good but it wasn't what I wanted. Sort of like a homosexual girl being in a healthy stable heterosexual relationship from one of those movies. Great relationships, but unsatisfactory. My family loved me but they had a lot of things they needed to figure out. Friends were never constant for me. Since, my childhood with the frequency at which our family moved no steady friendships were made. As you know, my mind is wired in a way that I am always ready for someone to leave. It may hurt but thats what happens. My love-life was confusing at this point of time but it hardly mattered. So, things hardly made any sense. There was no sense of belonging. No sense of love. No sense of achievement. There were constant reminders of how I hadn't reached my potential. There is just one thing you should learn my reader. Do not love someone for their potential, love someone for what they are at that point of time.

My therapist had a two hours talk with me the previous day. She told me that all I do is talk about the emotions of other people in my sessions. How they react. What they do. I never talk about how I feel? Why I react the way I do? Why do I not react most of the times? Why can't I tell Meera about the tiny things that bother me? Most importantly, she asked me something that I didn't have an answer to. I couldn't even think of an answer to this question.

"Why do you love Meera? There have been women in your life, there are other options you could pursue around you and there will be other women in your life if she's not around. What is it about Meera that you don't even consider any other girl as an option for a romantic endeavour anymore? What void are you filling"? She asked me.

Now, my reader, you know the story so I think I will leave it up to you to figure out what made me feel things unknown to me for someone who was unknown to me four months ago. There were somethings that were made clear to me after this conversation. I needed to think about my feelings too. They were important.

My feelings at this point of time was like the shit you hold for a lot of time. Once, you've held your shit for a long time, you are immediately constipated. I was emotionally constipated. No laxatives for emotions I guess. They just kept pouring out around Meera.

The day before I met Kartik, there was another really important insight I got from Hari. Now, Hari is a friend of mine who has consistently performed amazing feats in his education and career. Currently, he was working for one of the finest finance firms I knew. He seemed like someone who could give me genuine advice about my career.

"Bhai, I think I am good at what I do. Over time, I may get better too. It just feels like what I am doing is not worth doing. Like it is just about me passing time while feeling like shit till the day I die. What do I do?"

"I know what you're going through. Most people around me love these constant highs. Like they would do the same thing over and over again. They'd get better at it and it'd give them a high. For someone like you, you just need a few big highs in your life. For that, I guess, you just need to know that you'll be questioned at every step. People may call you worthless or even go to the stretch of calling you delusional. You just need to keep your strength and be certain of what you want. You need to be patient for the time it will take." Hari told me.

All these clear insights from the people closest to me in such a short span was what I needed to most. Now I knew what I wanted from my career. What I wanted from myself and most importantly what I needed from Meera. I just needed clarity and now I had it. It was time to take a deep breath and jump into the shallow sea of ambition for my career. It was also time to tell my family that I loved them. It was time to tell Meera about what I wanted and how to deal with it.

While drunk with Kartik, I sent Meera a message.

"I really really like you. And I can love the hell out of you. And I see that you need time. So do I. But it scares me. Also, when we get so close together naturally and you regret it, it hurts the hell out of me. It has nothing to do with your anxieties. It has nothing to do with our fears. I am not in this for the physical stuff, yes. But wo le deke ho hi jata hai. Kabhi plan nahi karte hum. And I really believe you like me too. I also believe you are a bit scared to face it. I don't want to force or rush you into anything. I don't want to hurt you. I just want to love you without hurting myself."

I immediately deleted it for everyone after sending it. Drunk texting never got anyone anything. Kartik agreed. Meera, had to take this decision on her own.

After my last meeting with the therapist, I ended up getting drunk with Meera. I had established boundaries in my head. No holding hands, no long hugs, no making out. Simple rules. Self control is a virtue. The amount of alcohol in your blood has a direct correlation with the amount of control you have over your basic instincts. Slowly subtly we were back to kissing on a busy CP street.

It then led to me kissing her neck in the back of a cab and ultimately a goodbye kiss under her house. Losing self-control was a bitch and a half. Although, It was so worth it.

Kartik and I, talked all night. We slept at four a.m. When we woke up, I realised one thing. I had to find things that meant enough to me so that I could gain some happiness from them. Meera, was one of them. She shouldn't have been the only one. The next morning, I woke up and called Meera.

"Do you want to meet up?"

"Yes, where do you wanna go?"

"Let's go have the milk-shake, I talk so much about."

"Big Chill Cakery?"

"Hell, yes."

"Okay, sure. Let's go."

Meera and I, were back to basics but something was different. She'd subtly suggest time after time that I was her boyfriend. I would question it with a hint of cunning.

We sat outside the cakery. I had said something sweet as fuck. Again. She held out her hand on the table so that I would hold it. We were two mature working adults in a teenage romance.

"You can't control this. Neither can I." I said.

"I know. It feels nice." She said.

"Why should we try to control it then?" I asked her.

"Let's not." She said.

"Does this mean you are mine? As in we're together." I asked her with the fear of love. I didn't mean mine in a way that I'd want to own her. I meant mine in a way that I could count on her and protect her with the same authority over each other. My heart was pounding harder than a pornstar's ass in a gay porno.

"Yes, Abeer."

•••

Warm Loving Medication

It's been a while since I've written anything. I usually write on cold nights with a cigarette in my hand. It's not been the same. Maybe because I had been a happier version of myself. Things with Meera have been running smoothly. Love-life for now was sorted. There was not a moment when I'd think about her and not feel my chest warm up. I believe it's human tendency to want more and more out of everything. The struggles were very different now. In between my brother leaving the country for higher education and being happy with Meera I was in ignorance. Ignorance that love was just an escape. Love is evil.

I had picked up Digital Art to pass my time in this cold winter vacation as soon as my brother left. Meeting my friends and family was just a task now. Entertaining them with humour was just a shallow chore. Nothing felt like anything. What I enjoyed the most, I enjoyed alone or with Meera. It was rare for me to be happy around someone else. It was difficult for me to be emotionally honest with anyone else. It was difficult to smoke cigarettes since I had a severe cold for several days now. It was difficult to go out and distract myself in this pursuit of misery. Meera was busy with her job and family. I didn't want to let her know that I was getting borderline suicidal. Living didn't make sense anymore. There is just one thing that I've seen in all the people I have dealt with. Holding on a bit longer usually helps. Especially in this scenario. I could not think of one thing that I enjoyed, that made me happy. Not one. I was tired of being sad all the time I was away from her.

Recently, I had slept over at her place since her family was out. We were just lazying around on her recliner couch watching a movie that I don't remember eating take out food. Thinking about love. After that it was my head in her lap. She was watching the movie and laughing. I realised I didn't enjoy anything like she did. I enjoyed looking at her face more. I lifted her t-shirt a bit and gave her post dinner pot belly a little kiss. She looked at me and I looked at her. She smiled wide. Like she always did. Maybe I loved her so much because it was a reminder that I could be happy too. She just started rubbing my forehead. Running her hand through my hair. Whenever she did that I don't know why I just felt so happy that I wanted to cry. Is that normal? Who knows? Wanting to cry is not a normal feeling for me.

Since so long I've had to be strong that crying was incomprehensible. My dear reader, I am sorry for talking about myself. But since Meera is happy now, this is all I can think about.

It was not unnatural for me to want to cry but the inability to do so. Some four years ago, my grandmother passed away. Hardly, mattered to me anyways. I know that's a very mean thing to say but it is my honest reflection of the kind of person I am My father was devastated.

All my sadness/concern came from the love I had for my father. Maybe just because how I detached I was, I was the right fit to handle my father in the absence of my mother. My grandmother passed away in Bhutan. Her last rites were to be performed at Varanasi. It was 22 hour drive. Sitting in a car with my father and grandfather for this period. With sudden outbursts of crying at random points of time. Don't get me wrong. Not my outbursts. Fore-mentioned were their outbursts. I was as blank and confused as a muslim feminist or a sufi extremist. I am sorry but I need my blows at religion to give me momentary satisfaction. I had never seen my father so vulnerable. It was the first time since I was 7-8 years old, that I hugged him. To comfort him, of course. I had an excuse. We were three generations of our family, trapped in a car for 22 hours thinking about different things. It was one of the most silent drives of my life. The same drive made a guest appearance a couple of weeks ago when we had dropped my brother and mother at the airport uncertain of his future and priorities after higher education. They were sobbing, again. I was feelingless, again. The last time I met Shivangi. It was again a late night drive. She was sobbing and I didn't know what to feel like. I wasn't attracted to her as a person I bet. It was the idea that she represented. Someone so young could be in so much pain. Maybe that's why I love driving alone late nights. The street lights passing by remind the most beautiful and melancholic times I could remember. Beautiful as in when she was watching the stars, resting her head on the window of a car door. The smile on her face. Love is complicated. Sometimes it makes you happy. Sometimes it makes you helpless.

The recent session in my therapy, my therapist straight up asked that if I had to define happiness in actions or feelings what it be. We had a minute of silence just for me to think. Finally, I could tone it down to physical affection, hope, a sense of belonging and a sense of care. Turns out it all four of these I never had before meeting her. Physical affection as in hugging her, holding her hand, giving her small pecks on her neck and eyes, her index finger tracing my fat cheek and her eyes looking into mine unhindered and luckily, certain. There was no confusion in her voice anymore. Just love and hope, as in looking at her made me see a better future. After a long time, I belonged somewhere. Her arms. I never felt like I belonged back home. It just felt like I was always fighting my battles alone. My parents were generous enough to loan me some money and love. It just didn't feel like they understood my battles. The time I told my mom about my anxiety her reaction was to make fun of it. I can't even tell my dad this because I don't know how he will react. Once upon a time, I told him I was suicidal. His response was that it was just an excuse for not studying. Home is where the heart is. Home is where someone understands you and doesn't belittles your issues. My parents did their best with the tools they had. I love them. It just doesn't feel like home.

Back when Meera and I were playing house at her place, there was a time when she had another episode of anxiety induced by vulnerability. She pushed me away, yet again and started crying/

shaking. I don't know what hit me. I started shaking out of the blue. We were on the opposite sides of a bed in a room as dark as the darkest of nights and most unexpected power cuts. She saw it as much as I tried to hide it. What she did made me love her even more. She wiped her tears and hugged me tight. She just told me, "It's okay, Jaan. I am right here with you. I will never leave your side." Something in me shattered. I just started crying. My face dug in to her neck, her lips on my forehead and her hands running through my hair.

Her voice as soft and vulnerable as it ever was and my mind as out of control as it never was. I had hated sleeping alone. After this, I will hate sleeping alone more. Maybe because I hated going to sleep sad.

My therapist after a two hour long session suggested that I take meds. Actually, insisted. I was tired of feeling like shit, too. It was time. It reminded me of a play I read. There was a kid who used to play out fantasies in real life. Sometimes he'd be a fireman, another he'd be a policeman and so on. His parents saw that as a dysfunction so they took him to a therapist.

"I think he has multiple personality disorder and mild bipolar disorder," said the therapist.

"What do we do doctor?" The parents were desperate.

"He just needs warm loving…" continued the doctor.

"Warm loving care?" he was interrupted by the concerned parents.

"No. No. Not that. He just needs warm loving medication."

•••

Birthdays

Last night I rushed to the emergency room, I believed I wasn't gonna be alive by sunrise. I didn't have my phone. I didn't have anyone there except my father. My father with his kind eyes being more heartbreaking than any love ever will be. I didn't know how I ended up here. I didn't know if I wanted to live. I just knew that I should've not been born. When you're born you just start having impact on people's lives. People start loving you and depending on you for their happiness. My life was now attached to Meera, my family, my friends and Bella. Someone once told me, "Write when you can't breathe without it." Today I believe, if I don't write this, I will kill myself.

My reader, my mental health has gotten worse. It has gotten worse to the point where nothing means anything. Today is 6th January. Yesterday was her birthday. The day before yesterday I met her family for the first time. The day before that I was at her place with her in my lap, kissing me like there was no tomorrow. I met her family, they seemed pretty sorted. Her friends her had known her family for years and years. I was naturally the odd one out. My anxiety was getting worse. I had stopped taking my medication because it was making me very aggressive and impatient. I would rather be in torment than get angry at Meera. It was a series of events that killed me. I was going to Patiala in a few days to work on career further on. I was insecure as to what would be with Meera and I, after that. Let's start at the beginning, eh?

It was the morning of 4th of January, I was on my way to pick up my girl. This past month was a series of long drives, stolen kisses and cliché music. It was all that I loved. I was still in the guilt of getting angry at her on the death anniversary of her father. The main reason why I stopped taking medications was because I couldn't see her cry again. I didn't want to fight. I just wanted to adore her. It just feels like I am not the same person I used to be. Whatever I do, feels so wrong. She asked me to pull over a nursery and very lovingly bought me ferns so that I could take them with me to Patiala. Then we went on to sit at a restaurant in CP to talk about what we usually talked about. She had taken a leave that day just to spend some quality time with me and I couldn't love her more.

That evening she was holding a party with family and close friends at Saket. She invited me too, even though she didn't want to. I was too immature to see that. It was probably too early for me to meet her family. They were amazing people. They knew how to work hard, party hard, be happy and make other people happy. Ideally, how people should be. The person I related to most was her elder sister. We talked about books, blogs and most importantly how clubbing feels like a pointless activity. I wasn't sure if anyone liked me. Her friends were very welcoming and I loved that. Her best friend killed me with her kind words about how she was happy that Meera was with me. People say all kind of things when they are drunk. There was a pair of earrings I bought for my girl with the suggestion of my mother. I wanted to give them to her personally to see the look on her face. I didn't get the chance. So I gave them the earrings in front of her friends.

All she said was,"But these are from your mom right? What did you bring?" I didn't know what to say because I didn't expect that response and no amount of her telling me how much she likes the earrings would ever fix that. The whole night I was there just because I thought Meera wanted me to be there and also because I wanted to be around my girl. Everyone danced for the whole night. I am a morning person so naturally I was ready to sleep. I headed home.

Her family very kindly invited me to sleep over at their place but I had to head home. My father was all alone at home. I wanted to be around him too but it was Meera's birthday so, priorities.

Meera had told me that she was gonna keep the 5th free so that we could spend some quality time. I had something planned for her. I was gonna start with Lunch at Dramz, Qutub. Then we were gonna head for evening tea at Hanuman Mandir. Then go to Bangla Sahib because she loved that place. By evening we would be at the terrace of Pragati Vihar looking at Jawahar Lal Nehru Stadium. I would kiss her a happy birthday. Pro tip never make plans for someone else's birthday unless you are married to them. Birthday's come with a lot of expectations from close quarters and what happens is things go down in obligations. Somehow, it felt like I was the obligation in this case. All the plans she made, she made with her family and then asked me if I wanted to come. I wasn't even a part of the decision making process. The thing I don't know if I got anxious because of the series of events or it was the anxiety that was making it feel bad. Either ways, I was disappointed. I am an introvert and I don't party much. I still would go to any party Meera would want me to be at. Emphasis on "want me." I can't stress how much I love most of friends. Her Jiju didn't like me much because naturally he's the father figure of the house. I just felt out of place there and I just knew Meera there. Somehow I talked to everyone else more than I could talk to her. In the thirty-six hours we were around each other for some eighteen hours and we talked probably for fifteen minutes. I loved seeing how happy she was. I hated being stared down whenever I looked at her. On the 5th I bought her a plant. A white rose. I wrote her a letter for her.

"I didn't know what you'd like." I am still not sure what it could be. I could've gotten you a perfume, maybe a dress or maybe a bottle of booze. In the pursuit of it being special, I couldn't bring myself to bring anything of my own.

Who would've thought I would straight up walk down the Aisle of that Indigo flight 6E 336 and talk to a girl who would change my life for the better.

What could be one possibly gift a girl that is a gift to this otherwise grey world?

From seeing you with your head out of a window and your back against the door, looking at stars.

You didn't know your eyes shine away more than any star.

From you looking super hot in that uniform to looking the most adorable kid ever in the nerdy t-shirts and glasses.

From you carrying the excitement and compassion of a kid in your heart and at the same time being one of the wisest people I've met.

You brighten up my life and nothing I could ever buy or acquire would ever give me that feeling.

You have no idea how precious you are to me.

You have no idea how much at one point I want to just run my hand through your beautiful hair while looking in your eyes.

You have no sense of how in another I just want to keep my head in your lap and sleep.

You have no idea how much I want to share everything that's precious to me with you. Without doubt without restraint.

Someone asked me last night, "How did you possibly woo this fine woman?"

I didn't know what to say. I just never thought of it as wooing you.

I didn't want to woo you, I just wanted to see and love you.

I just thought of it as living around you, enjoying the time we share and wreck the world a bit while we are at it. We are young, dumb and crazy babe.

You don't know how much I love myself when I look at you.

You don't know how much on that flight I just saw a strong face and sad eyes.

All I see now are these happy eyes. Mine and yours.

You don't know how many times I would get out of a Rajai to heat up a pizza for your hungry ass.

I love you more than I love walking in a cold street alone, smoking a cigarette.

I don't want to put this in words because words are meaningless when it comes to me and you.

I am not a party person babe, but I'll go to any party if that's the cost of seeing you.

"Happy Birthday, Jaan."

Somehow whatever I did just made it worse and she never had any reaction to any of it. I just needed something more. Some sign that yes she is ecstatic with me around her. She had zero reaction to the earrings, to the plant and to the letter. I didn't know what else to develop. It just felt like she didn't want to be with me anymore.

The night of her birthday she invited me to another club. We went we partied. It was exhausting to see the amount of guys trying to hit on her. It was exhausting how she'd barely even look at me. It was exhausting how I'd get stare downs when I looked at her. It was exhausting how I wasn't comfortable at a club and she didn't even notice. I had to go. My anxiety was killing me. I couldn't show it because she was happy. I didn't hate anything except the fact that my right leg and hand had been shaking for the last forty minutes. Either I was being a good actor or she was enjoying a lot. It was all very exhausting. To simply put it, I wasn't comfortable. I had promised myself one thing that day, that I'd never hide my feelings from her because her feelings usually lead to resentment. It was amazing how her elder sister would notice it and talk to me often. I love people who are observant and kind. But it was too exhilarating faking smiles, seeing the people hitting on her and drinking whiskey. I had eaten one meal in the past two days. So, I asked her to come out of the club and talk for ten minutes. I would go out to the washroom and wash my face hoping I'd stop shaking.

I just told her how I tried and I am not comfortable and I just wish we could get some quality time but it has passed. I didn't want to argue. I was too tired to fight. It escalated as it naturally would've. I was just too out of my mind to see any of it.

"You don't even realise, how much you've started fighting with me," she stated.

"I don't want to fight with you, I am just asking for your time." I said controlling the shaking of my voice.

"I don't have the time! What now?" She looked at me with the same look she had in that car when she asked me not to get serious for her.

"I should leave then." I said hoping she'd stop me.

"You should. Book a cab. I'll go once your cab is here. There is nothing to talk about now." She wasn't even looking at me.

I booked a cab. When it was at the gate she hugged me tight and stayed there. For the first time in an hour I didn't have to control my body shaking. It was her birthday. She deserved to spend it the way she wanted to. I was an asshole. I still am I just wanted this hug before things turned to shit. And they did.

I asked her to go since the cab was here and I couldn't control my shaking any longer. Once she went in, I fell to my knees and begged someone to help me. I don't know if it was God or myself I was asking for assistance. I took my two minutes. Then I went to the cab. For the past twenty minutes my heart felt like it could burst like a popcorn. I couldn't show her any of this. But I remembered my promise. So, I texted her that I was having an episode. My worst one yet. She called me and was on the phone with me for twenty minutes. I didn't want her to hear me losing my shit. I didn't want her family to party on her birthday without her. I could hear people calling her in the background of the phone call. It was my biggest fear. Her missing out on her life because of my condition. I just wanted to die. So that I couldn't hurt anyone anymore. It would be a one time pain. I always believed I was stronger than anything that came my way. Be at bad exams, bad presentations, toxic people, family issues and even criminals threatening me. I just always believed good things happen to good people. I was wrong. I told Meera I was fine now. She was very scared so I had to. She couldn't even do anything about it. If it was in her hands I would've told her. I wish she was there to hug me when I couldn't hold it together. I needed help for the first time in a long time and she wasn't available for that, family obligations and what not. So I sent her away. After we hung up, I fell on the floor shaking. Begging for some help because for the first time I couldn't stop it. It had been 45 minutes since I was in this state. I wasn't drunk. I wasn't sad, I was just me. Somehow my father saw me on the floor and he barely wakes up late at night. He took me to the emergency room. I had left my phone at home. I was ready to die. My eyes were fading, my head was light and I could just see the cold Delhi city lights passing by when my father drove me. I always counted on these lights to bring me peace, and they did. Hoping I could say goodbye to my family once again. I told my father that I loved him and that he is the best human being I know. I told him I wished we spent more time appreciating the positives we had rather than hating the negatives that we carried. This was the first time I saw him cry in my adult life. I don't remember anything after that except that I woke up on a hospital bed. My father looking over me with the kindest eyes he ever has. Not a bit of sympathy in them.

There was a lot of things I needed in life from life. I didn't know what. I didn't know when. I just knew that. If I didn't write this I would kill myself. I don't know what's gonna happen in life further on, I just hope it practices some self-control and gets a bit easier. After all, self-control is a virtue. Meera is calling me now, I don't know what I'll say when I pick up. Whatever it is, I'll let you know.

•••

Cowards

It was just a casual cold Delhi night. You know the time I so cherish. Summers were closing in. I'd have to hang up my sweatshirts and Jackets. I'd have to smoke less because smoking sucks in warm climate. I'd have to walk less because then I'd get my clothes dirty with sweat. Smelly clothes aren't good for social gatherings or professional workspaces. I somehow have a love-hate relationship with both. Certainly, like that one ex-partner you had who was beautiful when they were happy and out of control on the slightest hint of sorrow. Once you build a neutral perspective about things, you can't really hate anything, can you? You can't hate all the people who inflict pain on and on other people just to mend a broken part of themselves. You can't hate all the people in the world who bring hate into a conversation because now you understand where that hate is coming from. I don't remember the last time I hated something as much as I hate summers and my loneliness.

"I don't have many friends. I just know a lot of people," said Heath Ledger in a conversation with some random polaroid interviewer.

"I wish you get all the money and fame, you crave. So that you can understand that's not the answer." Look that up.

"Boom," said Kurt Cobain's shotgun.

Why am I telling you this? These people were as successful as most of us dream to be, why did all of them struggle with depression? Is it just because they didn't have a positive frame of mind? Kurt Cobain was the living montage of hell. His music will live forever even when he didn't want to. Jim Carey made masses laugh their asses off numerous times, what hurt his kind soul? He didn't have "real struggles." Heath Ledger experimented with drugs to such extent that he got cancer and he died a happy death. The same person who made teenagers pants go wild in his Rom-com roles.

No one has the answer to these questions because the only obvious answer we have is too hard to comprehend. Clinical depression is a thing. It's a thing to an extent where people have everything they've built with there bare hands, and still are not happy. We as people hate the obvious, because the obvious is the truth and truth kicks some hard ass.

All these thoughts were storming my brain while I was driving to Meera's place. It was Shivangi's death anniversary. It was hard to move on from the death of someone who was once under your care. You had one job. You failed. For the first time, I lit up a cigarette in my car and opened a window. I loved the cold comforting Delhi wind on my face, how real it was, how it'd play with my hair like Meera does. News flash.us Boys love being pampered too. Last night, Meera and I had a fight. It was difficult. Trying to save something we were obviously fucking up. Wasn't it a coincidence that Meera's father's death anniversary was one day before Shivangi's death anniversary.

The previous day, I made Meera cry for the first time and hence, the self loathing worsened. I loved when she smiled. I'd do anything for her to smile. Meera, had played a song for me.

A song that my friends listened to a lot too. She told me not to laugh over it but at the same time, I saw an Auto with Dekho Magar Pyaar Se poster on it's back. I had gifted that poster to a friend once because the dude never wore a belt. His ass-crack would always be visible. It reminded me of how much he laughed after he got that poster. So, I let out a snort. It was a fond memory. Meera, immediately turned off the music because I did the only thing she didn't ask me to do. I didn't know the significance behind it because I thought it wasn't that personal.

"Why do you always do this, Meera?" I asked. "Why is it always so wrong if I do one simple thing out of the situation?"

"It isn't that. I'll play it again…" She reached out for the aux cable.

"No. That's enough." I pulled off the aux cable. I didn't know the last time I was this angry. I didn't want to be that angry. It was not that big a deal.

"I just wanted to share with you my Mom's favourite song." She started crying. I had done something heinous. I had made her cry on her father's death anniversary over her mother's favourite song. Here came an episode. My body started shaking. I forgot how to breathe. I pulled over to the side of the highway.

"I am so sorry, Jaan. I don't know what took over me. I don't know why I did that…" I said, while shaking and I couldn't open my eyes.

She hugged me.

"You've recently started taking medication, Abeer. It's just that." She always had a golden heart. I was always the Demon people should run away from. No matter, what I did. No matter how I talked to strangers, I had a habit of hurting the people I love the most.

"It's not that, Meera. That's no excuse. I am just a bad human being…"

"Stop right there. You're the best one I've known. You don't have any problem with how I drink, what clothes I wear, when or who I go out with. I love being with you." She said wiping my tears off.

I couldn't believe two things out of the last statement.

Firstly, was the low how the bar was set on being a good boyfriend? I thought it was just being a good human being. Live and let live. I guess, Indian dudes have pretty much made sure that every person who doesn't eve tease, questions her character over her way of life and doesn't question her company is a good boyfriend. Well done, my friends.

Secondly, how could someone love me more than I hated myself? How could someone let her tears go to wipe off mine. How could someone appreciate me when I was the lowest status character of my own story? You know a lot of people live their whole lives without finding this kind of love.

Meera, always I assumed I loved her more than she loved me but it was times like these when she proved me wrong. It was times like these that fell in my unappreciative hands.

Last night's, events would give me shivers for all days to come. The problem with me is I never forgive or forget what I do. If I did, I'd do it all over again.

Today, I wanted to make her feel special. Her periods had just started and she sounded exhausted. So I bought her a nice bouquet of flowers, some Lindt dark chocolate that she so loved.

I went to her place. She hugged me tight as soon as she opened the door. Then came, her niece who was one of the cutest kids I had ever known. Something about Meera's family that I loved, they valued happiness over everything else. That was a huge leap coming from a family who mocked the happy underachievers.

What else I loved about her place was the Recliner Sofas. Just a couple of weeks ago, I was in Meera's lap on that sofa watching a mediocre Salman Khan film. I realised how ticklish she was, so I picked up her t-shirt and tickled her belly with my piggy nose. She'd just look down at me and smiled. She'd play with my hair. She'd run her index finger over my fat cheeks like a kid runs their hand over a puppy. Puppy love is delicious. She'd make me bite my lips and blush and I didn't know I could do either before I met her.

Today, she smelled the flowers. She loved them. I clicked her pictures with them, as she demanded. She loved that picture. I miss that expression on her face. I love her. Her niece, Hrida, was always excited me when she saw me. I don't know why. I come across as a violent person to a lot of people but kids never fail to be excited when they see me. I guess because kids know that a big beard doesn't signify criminal or moral issues. I wish more Brahmans thought the way kids did, there were so many times I was accused to be a Muslim like it was a bad thing. India needs to get it's shit together, like I had my shit together every time I made Hrida or Meera smile. Meera, had a guitar she always wanted to learn to play, I had a guitar far away and hence couldn't play. I knew Hrida loved music. Like aunt, like niece. It was a warm evening of laughing, singing and eating chocolates.

I felt like home with her. I felt like Home, in her house. I didn't know the last time I felt like Home anywhere. I wasn't a guest anymore. It was the biggest gift, Meera could give me. As soon as Hrida, decided to go to sleep I pulled up the recliner of the sofa and looked at Meera. She was so happy. I was so happy. As soon as Hrida, went Meera jumped into my lap and kissed me hard. She kissed me like there was no tomorrow. I had to take breaks to breathe. Cigarettes do that to you. And then she looked down on me with the intense affection that she carried for me. She'd make me want to cry. In a happy way.

I just kept her head on my chest and lied down, playing with her hair.

"I love it when you keep me to me like this." She said. I could not see her face but I knew she was smiling.

"I love it when you want me, to keep you to myself." I told her after taking a deep breath.

I had totally forgotten how it was Shivangi's death anniversary. It was time for me to go home. I started driving. I pulled out another cigarette and I lit it.

Funny thing, my reader, Shivangi's house was very close to Meera's. I would see it every time I was driving to or from. That day, I saw that apartments. I remembered the news article which stated that a sixteen year old girl had jumped off the terrace of her apartment, in Indirapuram. I instantly remembered the last conversation I had with her. How broken she sounded and how I couldn't help even if I tried my best. My heart raced. I started shaking again, and I had to pull over by the side. I texted Meera, she had slept. I pulled over to a cigarette shop and lit a cigarette. There was a girl standing there about Shivangi's age buying one too.

"Are you okay?" She asked me, seeing me struggling to light my cigarette.

"Me? I am super." I told her.

"If this is you when you're super, how are you usually?" She smirked.

"Oh! I am usually surrounded by people, so I don't have time to think." I smirked.

"What's on your mind?" She asked me.

"A friend used to live in that apartment and she threw herself from the terrace. I don't know if she was a coward or a victim." I told her, even when I didn't want to. I didn't know what else to do.

She was silent.

"What are you doing here so late anyway? It's 3:15 a.m. This is Ghaziabad and is it safe for you? Where are your friends?" I asked her.

"I don't have a lot of friends, I don't know a lot of people." She told me. I didn't know what to say. I didn't know what to do.

"Clinical depression is a thing. The people who succumb to clinical depression are called cowards. The people who succumb to cancer are called victims but how do you function when the only thing keeping you alive is your own worst enemy? Think about it." Then she walked away.

Seeing my condition, the shopkeeper offered me water. I told him I don't have more cash. He told me I could still have a bottle. Looking at the beautiful apartments in front of me sipping water, I could only ask myself. Was Shivangi a victim or a coward? What will I be called? Then my phone lit up.

"Have you reached? I love you." Meera had sent.

I was not dying anytime soon.

•••

Rock Bottom

"There's a client we need to launch in Patiala. As most of you are familiar with the city, would anyone volunteer to do the task?" asked my manager looking at me with the smirk on his face.

We were all sitting in an office down in Gurgaon. This particular start-up which recently started turning a profit treated us, the employees, pretty well if you asked me. The office was pretty lenient. At the end of most days, all of us would get high together and play poker. It was a funny way to keep the employees happy, but all of us were happy. Happy enough to stay. That's the thing with successful corporations, right? They continuously build a basic sense of achievement in the people who work for them. With a measly bonus and friendly environment, they make people feel welcome. It's only after sometime that employees realise that it's not such a friendly environment. Everyone is replaceable, everyone is expendable. Yet, people stay there because of the basic fucking appreciation and socialising they get to do. That's how life is too, you know. Most people these days, treat everyone around them as replaceable and it's true to some extent. I mean, people learn to live without their families so what's a work buddy, a friend or a lover? Remember the person you thought you couldn't live without? Look at you all living and shit, now. It's the harsh truth. There's no integrity left in most things these days, even love. To me, love was always a promise. It was a feeling, too. If you tell someone you love them, you see things through. If you tell someone they can count on, you mean it. The only regret I had at this point of my life is not keeping that promise to a friend and it cost her. The cost was Shivangi's life.

After this incident, the only thing I hated was my ignorance. All the while, I told her she could count on me. I was there because she was sad and lonely and quiet evidently, needed someone. Even after all the signs of her depression, subconsciously I believed that she was just a weak willed person. What I had for her was sympathy, not empathy. That's where it all went wrong. No matter how it looks, sympathy is never good. Not if you intend to stay in someone's life. There was a time when she shaved all the hair off her head. There was a time when she'd hookup with some questionable creatures just to feel something. There was a time when she'd want to cut open a vein and see what happens. It was all a cry out for help and all I saw was seeking attention. It was not her fault. It was mine. You're not responsible for someone's life but if you can save a life, you're a better human being. Even after all these signs, everyone close to her yours truly included didn't see it as an illness. That's the thing with mental illness. Every other form of illness is understood easily. It is easy to grasp the idea that someone has a tumour growing in their head but it is too difficult to comprehend how someone who has a seemingly perfect life, wants to kill themselves. I held Shivangi accountable for her actions. I pushed her away. I closed her off. I thought she might learn her lesson and live a better life. Also, I didn't want to see her kill herself. To some extent, it was easy to believe that she might be better off without me. That it didn't matter, if I was there or not. There were times when she lied to me. The last time she talked to someone, she told them that she missed me. That I made a difference in her life and she hated herself for pushing me away too. Oh that sweet sweet girl. She thought it was her fault that I was not talking to her. How beautifully naive could someone be?

"Why am I thinking about her in a meeting room?" I asked myself.

The answer was pretty simple, was it not? She's always there. She lives in my guilt and self loathing. She lives in the efforts I was making at the suicide helpline. She lives in my hatred to ignorance. If only I had known. If only I could comprehend that my life was saving someone else's. It's easy to think about what she did. It's easy to feel like the victim here. It's easy to blame Shivangi to ease my guilt but it was time to make the change.

"Alright, I'll do it. I'll launch the client, Sir." I said.

It was settled. I was the first one to volunteer and I was free enough to do it, at that time.

"You're the last person who'd volunteer for this, Abeer. Why now?" Shivam asked me after the conference.

"Maybe, I just need a change." I told him.

Although I hated Patiala more than being, I volunteered. Don't get me wrong, there's nothing wrong with the city. Patiala just reminds me of my misery. How it felt like I didn't belong here. That feeling never went away, it only grew. I just needed to take a break from trying to pretend to be happy in front of my family, Meera, my friends, my colleagues and strangers. It was mentally draining.

A few days later in Patiala, I had started regretting my decision already. I was doing something out of my comfort zone for a company that could replace me the first chance it got. I was doing it for money. Money is a thing too, isn't it? I can be a sulky little bitch sometimes. It's a personality trait I am working on. Each night after work, I'd talk to Meera if she was free. Each night after I talked to Meera, I would smoke a cigarette on a terrace and look at the sky. There was one thing about Patiala that was better than Delhi. You could see twenty more stars, probably. One particular night, I was doing the same. I was sitting on the terrace, smoking a cigarette. Suddenly, my hands started shaking. That was my usual deal. When a person can get used to anything, even anxiety. I got up from my chair, walked towards the door and before I could reach the door I fell on the ground. My chest hurt as if, it could rip open at any point. The same way, it was on the night of Meera's birthday. Suddenly, I could hear her voice, screaming.

"Do you want me to die, Abeer?" The same way she said it on the phone the night of my first major panic attack.

"I can count on you, Abeer. Just you." Followed Shivangi's voice.

These voices were constantly getting louder. These voices were killing me. So, I did what I thought was right.

I called Meera.

"Heyy…." I said. I was trying to pretend I was fine, I just wanted to hear her voice. It brought me comfort.

"Abeer, are you okay?" She spotted it just like that.

"Yeah, I am fine. I just missed you." I told her.

"You always miss me, idiot. I miss you, too. What's wrong?" She's cute beyond comprehension.

"Nothing, it's just another episode I think." I told her with a trembling voice.

"It's okay. I am here." She told me.

"That's all I wanted to hear, you know." I smiled in a panic attack. Mixed emotions are my thing.

I fell asleep after I heard this. I woke up after a couple of hours on the terrace of the guest house. I texted her. I told her I was fine. I had just fallen asleep. She was up.

"I am happy that you slept for once. I love you. Goodnight." She texted back.

Somehow, it still felt like this was not the end of it. There was no trigger to this panic attack. There was nothing overwhelming that happened to me then. It was just a random solid panic attack. It just felt like there were more coming, my way.

The next day, I had three panic attacks in a span of twelve hours. The day after that, something close to nine panic attacks in a day. It was time for me to head home. I wanted to be around Meera so that she could make me feel better. She always did, didn't she? The first thing I did, as soon as I went back to Delhi was visit my therapist.

"You've had a serious reaction to the medication." She told me.

"How could that be? I didn't take any other medication except this." I made my case.

"It happens, sometimes. The same medication that helps someone can have a reaction for someone else." She told me.

Was that just it? It happens. The same things could have different effects on different people? Isn't that the usual deal? If that wasn't the case why would there be dope-heads, weed enthusiasts and alcoholics? Since the history, we've known different things comfort different people. Some people like tea, some people coffee. Some people get anxiety because of weed, some people feel a calm throughout their body because of it. I was frustrated. Frustrated because I was tired of hearing this shit. I walked out of the door, never to go back again. Meera hadn't come to see me that morning. Anything could be the reason. My mind was too impatient then to understand anything. So, I accused her of not caring much about me. She came to see me still. She hugged me. I couldn't hug her back. I was too dumb for it.

"I am sorry, Jaan. I was very tired I didn't wake up on time." She told me.

Then it hit me. She had a late night flight. She came to see me after it. She must've been tired as hell. I hated myself more for blaming her. I had accused her of not being here because she didn't love me enough. I was too stupid to see that she was here. That's all that matters. Remember that folks.

We went to the bedroom, I just wanted to hug her and sleep. She seemed like she needed sleep, too.

When we entered the room, we cuddled up and slept. After a while, my body started shaking again. My face was away from her. I pulled my body away from her because I didn't want her to know. As soon as I looked at her, she was crying. She couldn't see me like this. I couldn't see her like that. I hated how helpless I was. I pulled myself together and I turned to her.

'I'll be fine. I'll be better. I'll try to be better." I told her.

"I just want my Abeer back. I just want it to be alright." She cried.

"I don't know if that's possible, Meera. You can break up with me if you want to. It's not an evil thing to do." I told her.

"No. I just want my Abeer back." She loved me.

"I promise you. I'll be fine. No matter what, I'll fight this. I'll make this better. I just need some time." I was shaking, still.

She hugged me very tight. Her tears ran through my beard. My hand went around her back and I hugged her tighter. I could never get used to it. Her smell. Her love. Who is this lucky? The love of their life, their crush, their muse loves them to this extent. I was stupid not to understand this. I was a sulky little bitch.

She was exhausted and she went to sleep. I was tired, too. I closed my eyes.

"Now you understand it, don't you? To be helpless." I heard Shivangi's voice.

I opened my eyes and she was sitting right there on the bed. She was looking at me, blankly. I blinked and she was gone.

•••

Love Hurts. Mental Illness Hurts More

To the people who have been in love with someone enough to beg, plead or even ask them to stay, I am proud of you. To the people in our society who enjoy sex enough to talk about it in a respectful way. Not as a brag, not as something gross but as something as a work of art, I am proud of you. To the kids whose love is being demeaned by every other adult who is sad in their own lives, I am proud of you. To the people who have love and lost to find themselves, I am happy for you. To the people who demean anything someone is passionate about, fuck off.

There was a general lack of passion in life for anything except my love for Meera at that point of time and I don't know why that was the case. Was it because I was sick? Was it because she brought me something I've never known? Isn't that what love is? Someone comes into your life to make you feel all the feelings you weren't even sure you wanted to feel? Feelings that usually sat in the back of your head, locked away in a dark room sitting in a corner waiting to be rescued by anyone but yourself. People in my life have always pleaded me to love myself, but how can I? How can I love someone who was ignorant enough to let someone around him kill themselves? How could I possibly love myself, when all my life I asked "what's wrong" and worked on it? In this process, I was somewhat good with academics. I could have a good career if I wanted to and I was into some forms of art. All I couldn't know was, why did she love me? Why did Meera love me? How could she? No one else ever could. My best friend now just called me when he had the time from getting high. He had new friends. My parents always looked at me like I am not the kid they wanted, that I should aim for a better career or a better life.

Somehow, I couldn't imagine a better life than the one in which no matter what I did I came back home to keep my head in her lap, give her pot belly a little kiss and fall asleep. It didn't matter how much I'd earn, what I'd do, all that matters is once in a while I'd go on a trip with her where I'd look at her eyes when she sees those beautiful stars. It didn't matter whatever the fuck happened in my personal life because I'd have a home to go back to. Where it will all be alright. Meeting her it was life like one of those YouTube videos in which a colour-blind person finds these special glasses that lets them see ever colour. There was so much more to life now.

Ever since, I was shipped off to Kota to be a better engineer than a human being I had only known one thing, disbelief. All my life I had everything I wanted except for a goal. All my life, I had everything I wanted except unconditional love and respect. Even my own mother at time would look at me like I am a monster because I was distant. I was distant because of my illness and because I couldn't let them know before.

Maybe, I was a monster. Maybe, I fooled myself into believing that I am half a decent human being.

"No woman will ever be happy with you. That's the monster you are." My mother told me on multiple occasions.

All I wanted to do was ask her what did I do? Respect my opinions and raise a conversation. Am I a monster for that? Maybe, I am Who gives a fuck? Meera didn't think so. All my life, I had seen women in my life struggle with their male counterparts and vice-versa. All my life, all I ever wanted was love not to be the power struggle it seemed to be. All my life, I didn't want to be like some of these men. These men would demean their partners to satisfy their parent's ego. These men would blame their ladies for all the bad shit going on in their lives. These men would blame their kids for not being up to their standards. The last thing I try to do is make someone feel unloved or undeserving.

Somehow, in our worst moments we become what we hate the most and that's what I had become. I was too blind to see, I was doing everything someone I'd despise would do. I was demeaning every effort Meera was making. I was questioning her love for me because it was hard to comprehend. I was questioning everything I had ever believed in. I was making her feel like she's not good enough. I hated myself more than I loved her.

There were two voices in my head, both of these voices at constant odds. You'll know what these voices would say sometime. I don't know myself at this point either.

On one of the worst days of my medication reaction, I was lying down on the bed on my stomach. It was about to begin. Whenever I was about to have an episode, the first thing that would happen was my lower back would start hurting. After that my arms and legs. The final point, the point where I'd want to die was when my chest would hurt. My heart would thump and my back would rise at just that point. It would feel like I was being pulled towards the ceiling with a metal fucking string attached to my heart. At this point, all I'd need was her on my side. All I'd want was her to hold me and tell me that she was there for me. That wasn't possible, was it? I would grab a pillow and pretend it was her. I would tell myself that it's fine. I would focus all my energy into why I want to live. How my parents loved me even when they didn't. How my mom would keep my head in her lap and massage my head. How my father would look at me with respect after all this time. How my elder brother and I would share an on-line game once he comes back from Florida. How I could go on another night-out with my childhood friends. How I could see Meera smile one more time. How I could make her laugh in that piggy way she did when I would make her.

In that moment when I was being manhandled by my own brain, I could see her face. I was about to drop her home.

"It's not working, Abeer." She'd tell me in a serious tone sitting on my lap.

"Is it not?" I'd bite my lip. I had never bit my lip before I met her.

"Yes. It's not working for you, you should just marry me." She smiled at me.

"Hell Yeah." I kissed her forehead.

It was my favourite part of dropping her home. When we'd just look at each other with all our heart and she'd just love me. The love I didn't deserve.

I was a sick man. Why should she sacrifice her happiness to take this responsibility? After all this time, all she needs is happiness. It was hard for me to comprehend the life she had lead but it was harder for her to realise that I was sick, too. Even after all the articles and blogs, she had read the way she talked made me feel as if she didn't comprehend it as an illness. That hurt. I could take the whole world not understanding but her.

When I was shaking on that bed, I looked at her. Not Meera. Shivangi. Shivangi lied on that bed like a carcass made out of agony and heartbreak. Her eyes were wide open and they were focussed on me. I looked at her with sheer regret. You know, how whatever you're running away from comes right back at you. Karma. Or Shivangi. I knew it wasn't my fault but I wasn't sure I did everything I could to help. Then her lips moved. I couldn't hear a word come out of her mouth. Things come full circle, don't they? It's beautiful in a way. How the universe works.

I am anything but a protagonist. This guy is made of mistakes, crimes and delivered pain. This guy is a selfish jerk on the verge of suicide who just wants to be loved. The love that could make him stop thinking this way. I was seeing Shivangi all the time these days. Each time, she'd just look at me with a blank look in her eyes that was impossible to read. With the same expression that a dead body would have. It haunted me for days and years and all I wanted to do was have Meera around me. She was the only person in my life who knew about Shivangi. She was the only person in my life who knew the real me. Every time I told people about my demons they'd run away. Every time I told her about my demons, she'd wipe my tears. She was my redemption and I was my own enemy.

The panic attack lasted for about an hour. So, I just sat up wore my boots and went on a drive. I drove up to Connaught Place, parked my vehicle and bought a cup of tea. Chamomile. It tastes like shit but some random high society people told me it's good for anxiety. While sipping tea, I'd sketch random strangers in the journal I maintain. At this point, people rarely surprise me. I always know somehow the scope of things they're gonna talk about. My optimism was long gone. My Nihilism was on peak.

Somehow, sitting there I'd like to make up stories about random strangers. What they could've been through and what they're gonna do by the end of the day. What kind of music they like and what is their poison of choice. It was late in the evening, Meera was supposed to meet me here in about an hour.

Time goes by fast when I sketch. She called me, I stepped outside the cafe. She came in for a hug. There was a different look on her face today. She was scared. I didn't know what of. I know, now. She was scared of what I was gonna accuse her of this time. I didn't disappoint. For the past few days, all we'd do was spend our time comforting Abeer. I was sick, I get it. She didn't have to suffer because of it. Get that. It's not a woman's responsibility to fix a broken man, this is not Bollywood and I am not Ranbir Kapoor. All I did was shake in agony and she'd hold me. Her heart would break over and over looking at me like that. I would stop if I could, I couldn't.

It's funny how someone can bring you all the happiness in the world and that person has the same capacity to bring in a world of hurt.

We'd keep on hurting each other. I was hurt because I remembered the way she talked about her previous lover and somehow, it felt like she was not over him. That didn't mean she didn't love me to her best capacity. It was good enough for me. It wasn't good enough for me when I was sick, when I was finding excuses to justify killing myself and doubting my worth as a human being. The reaction to the medication gave me severe self image issues, bipolar tendency, severe panic attacks and hallucinations of Shivangi.

All I wanted was her to hug me and tell me she was there. That she loved me.

All she had was fear on her face. Fear of what I had become. It was difficult to explain that this was not who I was. This was not who I had become. This was just me experiencing every pain I had ever felt at the same time.

•••

It's All in Your Head, Abeer

There is something about nights. I have told you I have a certain affinity for cold nights. You know why? Cold nights don't lie. They don't pretend. Cold nights come with the promise of loneliness and sorrow. It is the days that betray you. Everything is bright and shiny like my little pony but as soon as you turn your back, they destroy you. Sort of like Dolores Umbridge from The Harry Potter series, she would be dressed up in all conventionally welcoming clothes. Even her office would be decorated with harmless belongings but behind the facade she is one of the most hated characters in Harry Potter. She sends off the same vibe as say, Hillary Clinton. Nights are more like Severus Snape, They'd break you and make you but at the end you'll realise they were helping you all along. They helped you overcome your biggest nightmares. I am telling you this, my reader, because this was a night I was told something by a certain someone whom I thought understood me.

My reader, let me first tell you the highlights of my relationship with the girl of my dreams. I bet I have left out the good parts. I think we had established one thing way before we established anything else, Meera demands my happiness. She doesn't try to make me happy, she doesn't request me to be happy. She is just herself and nothing could feel better to me. She is that bright light of hope in that shit storm that is my self-hatred, guilt and lack of the will to live. I could live for her. There is something I understood about people who kill themselves after a girl leaves them, not that I'd ever do it. Maybe their life was unbearable way before they met the person, maybe life became a happier place after meeting them and as soon as they left, you realised life's not worth living either ways. Maybe these people bet their lives on the hope of a relationship working out. It is a pretty fucking stupid thing to do. You shouldn't live to be happy. You shouldn't live to feel good. You should live because the true value of a life is intangible and you are a fucking criminal if you neglect it. The way Meera has made me happy has been unreal. Those ultra warm hugs, those unexpected kisses and those unreliable drunken adventures.

There was a night when after a long long drive, Meera and I were talking in the car. I made a move and tried to kiss her. She played hard to get. Classic Meera. I stopped. Classic Abeer. I acted like I was upset in a teasing way. I put my jacket on my face and acted like I was sleeping. She snatched the jacket away from my face and she'd just come sit in my lap and kiss me. Kissed me like there was no tomorrow and if there was a tomorrow. There was a short window after that when she was just sitting in my lap stroking my cheeks with her soft, warm, caring hands and I would just be lost in her eyes. At that point I'd slowly touch her neck coming up to her chin and then cheeks. It honestly felt like hypnotism. There was a feeling that I can never explain. At the end of it, I just kissed her on her forehead, her cheeks, her eyes and her neck.

There was nothing in her heart, mind or body that I could be even a slight bit reluctant to explore. Her eyes felt like the most powerful thing I could comprehend. Even more powerful than the effect of Green Day on Emo Kids. Even more powerful than a tornado meeting a volcano. I preferred staying silent and looking in her eyes more than I'd prefer sex. I felt like a different man in her arms than I would in my natural habitat.

There was a time when Meera and I, went to a restaurant and as I was going to pay. She stopped me.

"You should let me pay. You've quit your job, now. Don't take anymore financial stress." She told me with a certainty in her eyes.

While this was not something you'd consider very special, it was very special to me. No one in the history of my friendships or relationships had ever told me not to pay without any special occasions. There were times I'd pay for my friend's birthday parties just to meet the bill because they were low on funds. To think about it, there were some basic things I had to worry about which I didn't have to worry about around her. Things were infinitely better. I felt protected for the first time in my life. Asking everyone else for help, felt like a favour. It usually is. She took the time to see the basic minor needs of me, which no one else ever did. It feels nice to be given a fuck about, you know. There are two things an adult can do if someone cares about them, they could take it for granted or they could appreciate it for what it is. Either ways, it would be amazing.

To pick up where we left off, the past two weeks have been a shit storm. A literal foolproof, with a few nuts on top, as smelly as Ghazipur on a rainy day - shit storm. I have no real idea of what is real and what is not. I have no real sense of what is fair and what is unfair. I have been very hard on the love of my life and not in a way I'd like to be. Things so petty started to break me. The things that would normally not even enter my mind. In the real sense, my anxieties had gotten way worse. The medication, the series of events and the heartbreaking realisation of a few truths got me down on my knees, begging for help. The panic attack I mentioned in the last story was gonna be one of many. I would not even realise how situation would go to be that bad. How it would hurt so much that I would want to die. But let me walk you through it.

The day after my afore mentioned panic attack, Meera came to see me. It was a dark dark evening I would rather not visit again but the things we have to do am I right. Meera, came to me with disappointment on her face. We talked. We threw around meaningless accusations of me being immature, her being inconsiderate, etc etc. Things we didn't mean. Things that had to be thrown up for us to be healthier. Things were made clear. Things that hurt, things that were meaningless because of the lack of emotion behind it. She told me that she was in love with her ex the same way I am in love with her. My sweet summer child. That is the last thing you'd want to say to your clinically depressed boyfriend. That hurt. Nothing she would say now can change anything about it. It has been fixated in my head. It broke me a bit. Like most of the things she did these days. She told me that the love she had for her ex was something that happens once in a lifetime. Still hurts. The only thing I could and can understand from it is that I am a compromise she had reached because things didn't workout like every other girl would feel like a compromise after Meera. She didn't love her ex enough to write a book about it. Modern day relationships huh. I believed Meera loved me as much as I loved her.

Very untrue, my reader. That is what life is, it is a mixture of small happinesses, disappointments and tragedies. Meera, didn't know what she did to me. She broke something in me. I felt like a loser to love someone, who would compare my love to her's for her ex. Who wouldn't?

My hands are still shaking when I think about it. These thoughts are still prominent enough, to want me to throw my laptop away and smoke a cigarette. Maybe a pack. Am I the rebound guy? Felt like it. I still kept my calm. Meera, in her ignorance about my condition didn't realise what she was failing me with word by word. I wasn't the same Abeer, she had met. I didn't know who I was anymore. Love can easily make you question yourself. It made me question a lot of things. What is the energy of this relationship?

What are we doing to each other? Why two strangers who met on a plane full of love for the world were now some strangers in a relationship?

"Abeer, I think you're too immature to be in a relationship right now. I can't handle everything at the same time. This is too much. I know how you're feeling. I have loved someone the way you love me. I know it must feel like you need more of my attention. You don't know how much it takes a toll on your partner. How it just kills everything." She said, "I know at your age stuff like this happens."

In one simple statement, Meera, my sun and my moon said everything she could to feel make me feel way worse. You don't tell your anxiety ridden boyfriend that you loved your ex as much he loves you. When you knows he loves you as much as he could, and more. Also, to demean my feelings because of my age was something that felt utterly tasteless then. I didn't mind. Why? Meera was the kid here. She had taken everything I felt and the way I reacted, as normal consequence of attention-seeking relationship shit. Meera had hurt me in as many ways as possible right then. I bet I had hurt her the same.

"You don't know how much I pushed him away. You don't know how much I begged for him to stay. He didn't." It was still about her and "lady-killer." That's what I am gonna call her ex this point forward. There are members in the society from both genders who have taken someone beautiful, promised to love them. Promised to make them happy and then left them in the dirt the first chance the going gets tough. We'll call these people Garden destroyers. Garden destroyers are like those kids whose parents don't teach them how to love and provide so what they do is they take a beautiful flower out of a garden and they pluck it. They want to own that flower so much that its dying doesn't make a huge amount of difference to them. Why? It's elementary, my dear Watson. It's because they know they could easily pluck another flower from the huge amount of gardens out there in the world.

These elements have a certain appeal to them. They don't have much personality but they trigger something inside you that it makes you feel the need for them. It hurts. It hurts like a motherfucker but they still can't let them go. They'd beg their tormentors to stay. Somehow they'd choose torment over the fear of loneliness.

Meera was an open book to me. I could see through the charade. I could see that she was too scared to love with conviction. I wanted to give her more time to figure that out. I was right here sitting on a bench of my colony after a night I went to the emergency room, still willing to hear her out and fix what was hurting her. She had all the love I wanted to see in her eyes but she disregarded it for immaturity. Well, good for her.

After she had said everything she wanted to, I was beta enough to tell her I'll try to fix my things. Why? My body was shaking again and I was trying so hard that she doesn't stop it. We fixed her concerns. We did everything we could. We then went upstairs and sat in my living room. There we talked more about how it was and how I was feeling. My dad was in the house but he just gave me space. The space to fix things. In some cases, when a person suffers from depression or anxiety they have two people in their lives. Ones they need space from and others they need to run towards.

Whenever Meera would have anxiety, she would push me away and whenever I would have an episode I would hug her as tight as I could. That's where I should've known where it went wrong. A person's subconscious always has the right answers. We are just stupid to see the signs.

After everything, she just went on to do something that reminds me one of my favourite movies. In this movie, there is a point where the leading lady in her ignorance keeps saying things to the protagonist in good will that trigger the protagonist so much he stops being himself. She means well. She means good. She just doesn't what to do with it. In the pursuit of trying to help the hero, she pushes him away to the amount where she begs for him to stay. She literally gets down on her knees in a graffiti ridden alley of Hauz Khas village to beg for him to stay. He doesn't.

"We can fight this, Abeer. Your depression and anxiety? It's all in your head." A bang went out in my head. My face changed. My face hurt. My eyes bled.

"You know, Meera, the reason I don't tell anyone about my condition is because I didn't want them to say this. I think you should read up about this because this is the worst thing you could've told me. I am strong enough to hear it from anyone in my life. My parents, my friends and my mentors but I didn't want to hear it from you. I didn't."

I stormed out of my own house not knowing how to feel and what to do. She followed me. I called the lift and was waiting for it. She kept her head on my shoulder. I couldn't look at her face. When you love someone, you discover a lot of expressions you never knew you had. For example, I never bit my lips but seeing my girl happy and giddy, I did that. This expression. The expression of utter disappointment and shame was killing me. I was ashamed of my condition and I was disappointed from her response. Shame and disappointment rarely come together in a person's head let alone on their face. My chest hurt, my head went blank and my face was down. My eyes couldn't see, my lungs couldn't breathe and my neck had no strength anymore.

When I entered the lift with her, she faced me. My head still down towards the ground. It felt like I was bleeding internally. My whole body was numb and in utterly disgusting pain at the same time. My spine tingled with agony.

She gently placed her hands on my cheeks and tried to bring my face up, to face hers. I was shivering because her touching me hurt like I imagined lava burns would. I wanted to die. My face and her face were on a level but my eyes were still down. She hugged me. She told me she didn't know. That she couldn't. I didn't know how to respond. I opened up with my deepest darkest secret to a girl I had always thought was the object of my salvation and she did exactly what she shouldn't have. In one evening, she had told me every possible thing she ever could and yet, I stood straight.

I was disappointed in her but not myself. I had zero exposure with someone's anxiety before I met Meera, yet I handled everything to my best capacity without belittling her pain. Does it matter if a person is drowning in a sea or 5 ft swimming pool? Drowning is drowning, right?

What Meera said to me was the alternative of someone telling an Asthma patient, "Why can't you breathe? There is plenty of oxygen around. It's all in your lungs."

Meera and I, stood in a lift struggling between compassion and disappointment. Struggling between love and care. Struggling between a desert and an ocean. We were in a super fucked situation where she would try to get close to me and my body would push back. This must've been the first time, my body was denying her touch and my heart was craving it. The areas of my body she'd want to touch (to console me) would go back on their own. She felt like acid, I felt like I was in misery. I didn't know what would come next. How do I love someone to my full capacity if they don't understand what I considered my only weakness.

The two minutes in an elevator felt like an eternity of altering between heaven and hell. Her arms being my peace, my mind being my chaos.

"I am sorry, Abeer. I love you, Jaan."

There I saw Shivangi, again. She was standing behind Meera, smiling at the utter irony of how life turned out to be. How I took her mental health for granted and what a bitch karma is.

Words meant nothing anymore. Nothing meant anything.

•••

To Each Their Own Agony

Panic attacks. You know from experience, what you feel during a panic attack a severe one is similar to what you think you'd feel if you were ever drowning during a heart attack. Now, mix that with a teaspoon of clinical depression and you have the recipe for hell. What if you were a great human being with amazing friends, beautiful parents, a competent therapist, a good job, decent drinking habits and a loving girlfriend but your only problem was your broken helpless soul? I learnt something the hard way, like most average human beings do, most of us modern day love bugs create our own problems.

There was a friend of mine who was so in love with a girl he had dated for years. This girl was what you call a modern day succubus but for him she was an angel. An angel straight out of the sky who fell into their sex deprived laps, an angel who filled a void created by the circumstances of their family, life and career. This woman came into their lives with a promise of paradise, a heart of gold and broken hearts. Broken hearts are the world's most beautiful aphrodisiac. Both of them meet up, help each other to come out of a dark hole called momentary eternal doom. In this phase, people feel like they have no future. They won't meet someone as amazing as their last partner so they settle for someone who makes them feel better about themselves. Who sees them like they couldn't see themselves. People have the guts to look into their own souls, find the little crying kid and tell them that life is not worth it. This friend ended up killing himself. This friend thought that their life was worthless because their partner left them. My friend begged them to stay, to reconsider their choices. My friend was suffering from clinical depression for years now. They were a good student, an amazing human being, a pure soul and someone who would help strangers. Why did their partner leave them? Mental illness is overwhelming. With any other illness, people stick together because they know that their partners appreciate their company. With mental illness, it's hard to establish if your company is actually helping the patient or not. Their head is their own prison. People like these could feel like they were trapped in a box when they were sitting in a room with their loved ones and they'd feel at peace sitting alone smoking a cigarette. Most of the people in our generation have certain mental illnesses that would hurt their life in every possible way. Be it career, love life, family, friend circle and mostly their peace of mind.

So where do all of these members of our society fuck up? From most of the people that I've met, including myself, fuck up by counting on that one person that feels comfortable enough. What we don't realise is that person may have issues of their own, they may not have the mental or emotional space to handle your issues. The strongest of people have once in their lives gotten on their knees for love. As soon as they got on their knees, love left.

Meera and I, were becoming strangers. My panic attacks were getting worse day by day. Her heart would break seeing or hearing me like that. In my problems, I had forgotten she suffered from anxiety herself. She was scared of love when I met her and our love was reaching the conclusion she was always scared of. I would expect her to see me or call me when I was having my panic attacks but I had forgotten she was suffering too. She was suffering and she was being very strong. She had to maintain her family, her job, her friends and a sick boyfriend. Times like these are very testing. They make people forget the best of times. They make people hurt so much that they forget what happiness was. I was at a point where I was having panic attacks three to four times a day. My anti-depressant medication had reacted. I was at a point where I'd hug her and shake for hours. At a point where I'd see her with resentment even though she was doing all she could. There were points even though, I was saying something else she'd understand something else. She was the only person I counted on. The only person who could comfort me at that point. The only person who could touch my hair and make me feel a thing. What I hadn't told her was that I hadn't had a proper meal in weeks. That I used to walk for hours without feeling a thing. That I'd have cigarettes after cigarettes and not feel a thing. The things I used to love, I hated now. Sitting with my family was a task on it's own. There were times I would feel so hopeless that I'd want to commit suicide. I had everything and yet I felt like I had nothing. Therapists and medications, felt like a waste of time. God felt like a sad little joke and there was no light at the end of the tunnel and if there was, it must've been a fucking train.

There were times when she'd come to my place and wait for me to come and my concern would be that she didn't come sooner. There were times when she'd give me all she had, and I'd ask for more. I could say I was sick but there is nothing that I regret more. The girl I loved, the girl who made me the happiest and I made her efforts feel worthless. The unhappier I made her, the more I hated myself. I knew she'd be happier if I didn't get sick. I didn't give her own space. The space that I had never evaded.

There was a time Meera and I, sat in my car and talked about everything. She'd cry and demand her old Abeer back. The Abeer I missed too. The Abeer that made her happier and hence, made me happier. I promised her I'd get him back. She believed me. I believed myself too. Abeer, had now become this stupid fuck who had made Meera his therapist, best friend, family, home and salvation. That's a lot of load for anyone. People are not strong enough to be an anchor for lost souls. That's why we created the idea of God. Someone who could handle everyone's pain and sorrows and not feel a thing. No wonder he is imaginary.

Meera was unreal too. The best thing about her was she never showed any love for materialistic things. She only valued happiness over every other thing. Her eyes would still sparkle like the sunlight falling on the snowy mountains of Kashmir. Haminastu. The series of events that followed were neither her mistake nor mine. It was just unfortunate circumstance. I had lost myself. I had quit my job, I was not writing anymore, I was not hanging out with my best friends, I was not spending time with my family, I used to have panic attacks and I'd wait for Meera to text or call. The only thing I'd look forward to then was seeing her face or hearing her voice because that would bring me peace in utter hell anxiety and depression created together.

My body gave up, my heart felt like it could blow at any moment and my head would feel like the biggest void. The more I had anxiety, the more her heart would break and the worse my situation would get. Maybe all we needed was a break. I couldn't let her go at a point like that. She couldn't handle my pain at the same time. Whenever I'd have anxiety, I'd want to hug her. Whenever she'd have anxiety, she'd push me away. My way of dealing with it was with her, her way of dealing with it was breathing in her space. I was very scared because I wanted to kill myself. There were two voices in my head constantly, one would say everything was great and everything was fine. Another would say, everything is just a broken bottle of fine wine.

There are a lot of things I wish I hadn't done. The voice that would think everything was crooked, would also make her feel worthless, her actions unappreciated and her company useless. That voice was temporary and I was fighting it with all my might. The other voice would want to hug her and thank her for all the things she'd done. All the sacrifices she had made and all the love she gave me. The two voices were at constant odds. Now there is only one voice. The voice of logic.

I also wish I hadn't had gone to see her that one last time because I somehow knew it would tear us apart. After weeks she was taking her own time and I fucked that up too.

I went to see her to give her some chocolates that would go stale. Chocolates, I knew she loved. I went up to her and I wanted to talk to her. The previous night she had a party with her friends. At the same time I had a four hour long panic attack after which I passed out on the floor. She couldn't have known what was happening and I didn't want her to know. It would only hurt her more. The next morning since I woke up my body was shaking and my heart was sinking. I had to go see her. So I made the biggest mistake of my life. I pushed something and it broke. We can call it my weakness or we could call it my sickness. Either ways, I broke her and my heart.

"Meera..." I was shaking. "I don't know what the fuck is going on in my head these days. I can't spend time with my family. I can't enjoy the company of my friends. I can't do anything that I used to enjoy. No matter what someone does for me I feel like I need more. I hate myself for that but I don't know what to do with it, Jaan. I just don't want to feel bad anymore."

She was silent. I wanted to know what was in her head. She had stopped telling me since she was terrified of what reaction I'd have. I understand everything now. I only wish I did, then.

"Say something, na." I pleaded.

"What do I say, Abeer? When I see you shaking I feel like crying. I feel like shouting." She shouted at the top of her capacity.

"So, shout then but at least tell me what's going on." I didn't know what else to say.

"I don't want to be in this relationship, anymore." she seemed sure.

"Oh. Okay." I saw it coming a mile away and I couldn't help but push it. It was like an itch I had to scratch.

"I am not getting my space. I just wanted to spend this weekend at my families. You couldn't let me have that too. I leave my family, my niece to see you and nothing is enough." She was crying and shouting.

"It's okay, Meera. I'll learn to be more considerate." I tried to touch her elbow. It was too late.

"Don't touch me!" She pulled back. She was shaking. She was crying. I didn't know how to respond.

"I've to go, Abeer. I have to go. I suggest you go home and sleep it off. That's how I try to feel better about things."

I asked her to let me drop her but she stepped out of the car and started walking. I tried to stop her. She wouldn't.

She turned to me.

"Everyone always told me I wasn't good enough. I didn't want to hear it from you, Abeer" and she walked away.

What had I done. I had promised myself to love this girl. To always let her know what she was to me. The other voice in my head had won. It was gonna die soon but like every good villain it did the most damage to me while going. How could I tell her that I never meant she wasn't good enough. I wasn't good enough. She was everything I had ever needed and I was everything I had ever hated.

I blacked out. I woke up on the walkway. The shopkeeper outside her colony who was always kind enough to let me have free cigarettes woke me up.

"Are you okay?"

"I don't know."

"It's okay. Girls come and go."

I laughed so hard. Girls come and go is another lie we tell ourselves to hide our shortcomings to hide our pain. Who else would I find to hold my hand while I was driving my car? Who else would I find that would look at me and make me feel like the most adorable thing ever? For your information, I am a bulked up dude with a heavy beard, a stare that would scare quite a few people. I'd never felt adorable. It's a "Fuck Yeah" feeling.

It was funny how in a trying time Meera and I, had forgotten all the amazing things we had gone through.

How I'd play guitar for her niece on a video call. How I'd wait for her in the car for hours sometimes after her flight. How I'd get her chocolates when she had her periods. How she'd sit in my lap in my car, looking in to my eyes with all the world in her eyes while stroking my cheeks. How I brought her flowers the one time, the flowers she loved. How we would paddle our legs in a kiddish way at a red light. How I'd keep my ear on her tummy, and hear it growl. How she'd have her head on my chest, me stroking her hair and I'd just keep her to me.

How I'd drop her to the railway station early morning after four hours of sleep because I had to spend time with her the previous night. How she'd leave her family to walk in the streets of Shipra Suncity with me. How she'd lie on my back naked and whisper things in my ear. How I'd put my head on her lap and go to sleep looking at her face. How she'd make me feel safe when my mind couldn't do that for me. How one time I fell asleep while making out with her and she laughed so hard. How she'd love me when I couldn't love myself.

Girls come and go, yes. Girls come and go for people, who never dared to love. Maybe I'll move on too. I'd have to. It's a world of pain, life. I had been fighting clinical depression for years, now. I could fight heartbreak. The only thing is I wish she didn't believe the other voice in my head. I wish she believed the real, Abeer. I kept my promise to her, I brought the old Abeer back. It took a lot of guts. The only problem was she didn't want him anymore. It was too difficult to gather the courage, after what had happened. My friends tried to set me up with all kinds of women. Artistic, religious, nihilistic, idealistic, realistic, etc. Every time I'd just end up telling them my story. There could never be another, Meera. Meera, told me once that she could never match my level. I told her I couldn't match hers. She was my muse. I found a very mediocre poem I had written before we got together.

"There was a girl in a flight,
A pair of eyes sad enough to freeze the sun,
A set of lips holding on to stories beyond my comprehension,
All I had was a laptop to work on and pictures to edit.

There was girl in the back of a cab,
A girl with a heart full of sorrow,
A head full of fears and hurtful words on her lips,
All I had was affection in my eyes and disappointment in my heart.

There was a girl drunk enough to dance to every song that came once,
A girl brave enough to trust a stranger,
A girl with a smile on her face as bright as the sun itself,
All I had was ankle cast and eyes that didn't wander.

There was a girl who looked at the stars with eyes that sparkled better,
A girl whose hair flew adding colour to the air it flew with,
A girl who held my hand and life was colourful again,
All I had was a need to not let go.

There was a girl who sobbed at a concert,
A girl who wanted to see the stars with her father once again,
A girl whose eyes cried and lips smiled,
All I had was helplessness as to why I can't help.

There was a girl who looked at everything with excitement,
Excitement that could make anything beautiful,
A girl who was art herself,
All I did was be the curator.

There was a girl who needed stability and adventure,
A girl who was meticulous with everything she did,
A girl kind enough to sacrifice for a stranger,
All I had was a cynical mind.

There was a girl who would come to our tent and put her head in my lap,
A girl who would hold my hand and say, "Shhhh."
A girl you could hold in your arms and all nightmares would vanish,
All I had was love to offer.

There was a girl I kissed at a concert,
A kiss that you don't forget,
A girl who regretted it,
All I had was dreams and pack of cigarettes.

There was a ring that I found in pocket of my jacket,
A ring that belonged to the girl,
A ring that wasn't important to her but meant the world to me,
All I had was a thread to wear around my neck."

•••

Flights and Therapists.

"Can I talk to Meera? Maybe it'd be helpful for your sessions." Damini said.

"What do you wanna talk about? There's nothing you can tell her that she already doesn't know." I was firm.

There were so many people around me who had approached her in some way or the other to talk. Why wouldn't they? I was the definition of a fucking mess. I am still the same old mess. Hiding it is way easier now. The same as her, I don't talk about my feelings anymore. That makes me a happier human being. Anyway, there is no one around me who'd understand why I still love her. Hell I don't understand it. Sometimes there's no logic to things. Like if you ask a five year old, what's their favourite colour they'd probably not be able to name the colour but they'll still have a certain love for it. That's how the world worked now. That's how it has always worked. You just love things for what they are, without adulteration or alteration. That's why love is the most complicated word in the history of time.

I went to Damini, who had been my therapist for months to help me understand the reason I loved her and get rid of it but instead she went on the same track as everyone else. She wanted to bring her back to my emotional proximity but that's where she's wrong. You shouldn't have to beg people to stay. There are a lot of things we shouldn't do, but we do it anyway. Why? It feels good to break a few rules sometimes doesn't it? For example sometimes you just gotta have a cigarette in a no-smoking area. Sometimes you just gotta get drunk on a Monday morning before work. The white girl equivalent to it would be going to work without a Venti triple Caramel shot fuck-iccino in their rich hands. The brown girl equivalent to it would be sneaking out at the night to go partying or maybe to not pay dowry in places like Uttar Pradesh or Probably have a smoke in the public. Damn, people have it hard.

"I just think I can talk to her and make her see your point of view. That you're not as a bad person as she thinks." She said.

"I am going to stop you right there. I am much much worse than she thinks. She's just blaming me for not having our privacy, and your solution to it is go talk to her about it? Meera and I are very different people but the one thing we have in common is we don't like people's opinion in our decisions. That's what I love about her, she doesn't give in to peer pressure. So, this… whatever this is, isn't going to do anything to help. Also, why'd you think she cares? She didn't care about my mental health and suicidal tendencies when she left five months ago. Why'd she now?" I was aggressive but I couldn't hurt her more. Whatever the cost.

"Okay. What should we do then?" Asked Damini.

"Who's the therapist here? Anyway, What I should do is make a life that is better than whatever this is. So that If she comes back someday, I don't push her again. If she doesn't, I'll have a better life wouldn't I?" I told her.

"Okay, makes sense. How'd your date last week go?" She asked.

"It was good. The girl was pretty fun to be around and the good thing is she is an insomniac too. So I'll have someone to talk to on lonely nights. She can be a good friend, but it isn't the same you know." I lit a cigarette. Fuck, I love outdoor therapy.

"So, what all did you guys do?" Damini was amused. It was funny how she was always amused when I talked about women.

"We went to the Starbucks, then we realised we could have coffee at 9 pm or we could just go grab a few beers. We ended up drinking a hell lot more than either of us could afford, then we just danced. Something told me she wanted to hookup because she'd just try to get closer and closer." I told her.

"So, why didn't you?" She snickered a bit.

"The last time I came even close to that, I called her Jonu." I felt bad.

Damini was silent. She did that when she knew I had something more to say.

"I don't want to kiss a stranger while I miss someone else. I know how it feels to be on the receiving end of that. Also, I am scared of love and what it does to people." I finished my cigarette.

"What do you wanna do then? What do you want to do that will make you feel good?" She asked me.

"I've considered driving my car into the wall, maybe then she'd care a bit." I was sarcastic. Or was I?

"What I really want to do is buy a bike that has a single seat and be on the move all the time. I've started volunteering at Bangla Sahib so that's good. I probably want to spend some time with my baby cousin. She's here only once a year. It's different with her too now. She always asks me if I am okay. Kids see a lot of things that adults choose to ignore. Uma and Hrida are probably my favourite kids in the world. Also, catch the flight tomorrow morning."

"So do just that. Also, have fun while doing it." She thus ended our session.

On my way back home, I saw the same lights that this Poem of a city had for all of us. I could never get bored of it. What I could get bored of was not letting go of Meera. All I had on my mind was the flight I had the next morning. It was the same airline Meera worked at. Even thinking about the uniform would send me down a bad trip. Around 5 months after I had seen her, I travelled in the same flight again. I just realised I've been avoiding flights to my best capacity. Even the thought of a flight would remind of the day I first saw her, being beautiful and all. Have you ever wondered why most of have trouble moving on mostly when the other person is so pretty that it makes your heart melt? Every person I have met before and after Meera, is barely like her in any way. I have been on a few dates after meeting her but none of them could make me feel that warmth in my chest. You know how sometimes there are a few itches you gotta scratch? It doesn't matter if it's gonna leave a mark on my body or not, all that matters is that you gotta scratch it. Meera was that itch now. Nothing and no one could replace what she gave me. At the beginning go this year, I had everything I ever dreamed of. I had a first draft of a book, Meera by my side and a will to live. Now, I just have seven empty boxes of cigarettes in my bag. Also, a few tattoos. In these months, I had lost 14 kgs by necessarily not ever being hungry. I never drowned my sorrow in Alcohol, although I did smoke my sorrows up. I even joined a boxing gym to feel more powerful, but it didn't matter how powerful I became I would be on my knees infant of her. I was more attractive to women now but how did it matter? I don't know why women love a good emotional mess, maybe it's because they want to nurture someone into a good loving human being. Or maybe, emotional messes were just easily manipulated? Who knows? What I know is my mind these days is running in every direction doing everything it can to avoid things that were important. Like food, water, career and human kindness. If you think my self hatred was at it's peak before, look again.

Just when I was about to reach home, my phone rang. It was Sameera. Now, Sameera was a junior from college. She was one of those people who had a toxic home and a kind heart. Just the combination I like. So, I picked up.

"Hey stranger." Sameera seemed happy after a long time.

"Finally." I smiled.

"What?" She asked.

"You seem so happy after months of knowing you. Did you get laid?"

"No. Better."

"Mary Jane?"

"Better. I landed a better job."

"I guess congratulations are in order." I was genuinely happy for her. Nothing like people rising above the toxicity of their lives.

"You seem happy too."

"Yes. I am going to attend a friend's wedding in Egypt. Have a flight to catch in the morning."

"Well wish him the best."

"Her. but I will."

"Did you ever wonder what could happen between us after that adventure we had last month?" I forgot to mention. We hooked up a few times. Funnily we would never talk when we lay in bed. It had been so long since I had done that.

"Yes. We'd probably get tired of each other's shit and go back to our Ex's." I laughed.

"Would you? After everything?" She seemed curious.

"Probably." I was serious.

"More importantly, we don't have the basics. We don't love each other." I told her.

"What makes you sure?" She asked.

"If you love this. Whatever I have become, you'd probably need therapy in some time. I don't know what I am gonna do the next day. Also, this isn't the right time to fall in love with me. I am being honest."

"Anyway, I have a flight to catch and hence, some packing to do. Can we talk when I am back? I am sorry." I told her.

She seemed disappointed. Reality is often disappointing.

Did I tell you that Meera and I stopped talking because people around me wouldn't leave her alone with the "Abeer was on medication" talk? It's probably because they saw it and I didn't. I missed her. I never talked about her. I deleted all her pictures. I was happy in my life and I was growing. Isn't that what love is? Missing someone when you're unhappy is easy. Missing someone when you're happy is what matters. I'd probably be happier if she kicked me in the balls than I am without her in my life. Sometimes when I went to sleep I'd still imagine if I had her arm under my head. The way she smelled, the way she laughed and most importantly, the way she looked at me. No one could ever look at me like that again. But who gives a flying fuck? Whenever I missed her, I went out and raised some chaos. Life's good with chaos.

But tonight, I had to sleep. Dreamless slumber is not something, I'd characterise my sleep as. It was more like endless agony.

"Get up, dude. It's 12 p.m." said Vikas handing me a cigarette. I was at our place. Everyone was there. Akash, Aditya, Vikas and Abeer. The sausage party.

I woke up. Looked around. Everyone was looking at me. I lit a cigarette. As soon as I did, there was knock on the door. Everyone looked at me.

I groaned, walked up to the door in my jeans and no t-shirt. I opened the door.

"Meera?" I said rubbing my eyes. I was shocked. She still looked as beautiful as a day-dream.

"Don't you live your life too casually for a 27 year old? You've lost a lot of weight. Just because you published a book and it did well doesn't mean you let your life go down the drain." She told me smiling. Still as assertive as ever.

"It's been 5 years and this is the first thing you want to tell me? How I am destroying my life?" I told her taking another puff. She was silent. A bit upset too. I decided to lighten the mood.

"Anyway, what brings you hear? Did you want to be around someone who loves you so much, you don't have to love them back?" I was not good at lightening the mood.

"Loves? Not Loved?" She smiled. Somehow my cynical remark worked.

"Yeah yeah, Potato Potaaato." I smiled back.

She hugged me.

"I loved you. It's up to you to believe it." I didn't know how long I had waited for this moment. After all the women, I had hooked up with. All the women who just wanted me to love them, I still loved her. It was a loser move honestly. It's okay to be a loser for just one person I told myself.

She let go.

"You never notice yourself, Abeer. As soon as, I stop hugging you it's like you stop breathing for a moment. A part of your soul leaves with me." She told me stroking my hair.

"Aren't you married? How does it matter how I feel?" I asked her and myself.

"Just because I am married doesn't mean, I can't see you." She told me with a firm cute voice.

"You have nice tattoos, now. What do they mean?" She asked me.

"Do you really want to talk about my tattoos? What brings you here?" I said in a teasing voice biting my lips for the first time in 5 years. Fuck I love her so much.

"I just wanted to see you. It's been long. I missed you." She told me.

A part of my heart melted. A part of my soul came back. It had been so long since I wanted to hear that.

Just before I could say anything, Vikas budged in, "Aren't you gonna introduce us?"

I gave him a serious look.

"I take it, you're Meenakshi. He just calls you Meera, now. The name hurts him too much." Vikas told her.

"Dude, why don't you fuck off?" I told him smiling in a way only we understood. He gave me a wink and walked away.

I led her to the balcony. Offered her a seat. Went in to get a t-shirt. Got her something to eat.

"What makes you think I am hungry?" She was smiling like a kid again.

"You're always hungry." I told her.

"You sure do remember the details." She couldn't stop smiling. Good memory is a bad thing. Especially, when you want to forget.

After she finished eating, she told me she wants to meet the people I live with. I could never say no to her. As soon, as we entered the apartment they were blasting the songs I sang around Meera. The songs I hated, now. Vikas would always tell me to stop feeling the music I hear. I couldn't do that. After Meera left, I'd either listen to Hip-hop or Classic rock. Least romantic songs, preferably. When I'd miss her, I'd only listen to "Tum ho toh" from Rock on.

We chilled for a while. One of the things I loved about Meera was that she could talk to anybody with zero awkwardness. She was chilling with my friends. I was just hearing them and laughing. I realised I hadn't smoked in the past two hours. I didn't feel the need to.

After hours of talking and laughing, I sat alone with Meera. I saw a bruise on her left eye.

"How did this happen?" I asked her.

"I fell.... in the bathroom..." She told me. I knew a Black eye when i saw one.

"Who hit you?" I asked her.

"What do you care, Abeer? What's in this world for you anyways except pointless pussy and misery?" She got defensive.

"I am not the one with the Black eye." I told her. She was silent. I knew her. She wouldn't take shit from anybody. Why was she now?

"I... I found a guy. He was a gentleman. The kind I always wanted to be around. He loves me." She told me.

"Look, I didn't have a say in your life when we were together. I sure as hell don't have one now. I just know this. If someone loves you, they don't hit you. No matter what." I said.

"He'll be better. He's just going through a rough patch. He'll be fine. I'll make him better with him my love. He was drunk." She resisted tears.

"Hey. It's gonna be okay." I told her.

"Anyway, it's still better than how helpless you made me feel with the excuse of depression, anxiety and the so called medication reaction. He made me happy when you made me feel helpless. We met around that time..." She was still defensive.

"I don't want to hear it." I interrupted her. I didn't want to know she had broken up with me because someone else made her happier. I didn't want to remember her like that.

She was silent. She looked away.

"You can justify abuse but you can't justify my sickness?" There was a sorrow in my voice I couldn't understand. I was going to faint.

She looked me, dead in the eyes. She looked at me with the same cold eyes she had looked at me all those years ago in a cab when she asked me to not get serious for her.

"Yes, I can justify it because he's worth fighting for." She broke me. I heard the sound of metal banging metal.

I'd rather have her kick me square in the balls. Anyway, I woke up. I was on the sofa. I guess that's how you can tell you are an adult. As a kid, whenever you sleep on the sofa you always woke up on your own bed. Now, you just wake up where you slept. I took the cab to the airport.

The world was very different now. A celebrity committed suicide this morning. Nonetheless, a young handsome actor. It was weird how everyone was an advocate of mental health on social media now. Even Meera. That's where things go wrong for people. They are sick and they expect people to stick around. They never realise that all you have is yourself and your family. The same people who hurt you will later on turn a page in their lives and start believing in things they never could for your sake. My family and friends would always tell me how it was her fault and I would always defend her. I wouldn't let anyone talk shit about her. Seeing this I realised that maybe I was the fool, here. I was sick and I could've been better. I tried my best. There were friends who had suddenly stopped hitting me up because they knew I was not the same happy go lucky asshole who would go drinking with them and laugh my heart out. They knew something had changed in me and they did not want to stick around until I pulled my shit together. That's an advantage of a breakdown. You know who is always by your side and who is there for just the good parts. That's where the truth lies. The true feelings of a person is revealed in the most difficult of circumstances. I am grateful for the people who sticked around. That's what life is all about; The people who stay. I had the purest of feelings for Meera. I hurt her, yes. I could've been better. I did not get a chance to get better with her. I was better now without her. In this whole battle, I am proud that I did not try to take my life. I wouldn't want to be known as someone who killed himself over a girl. People wouldn't see the years of depression. All they would see is that I lost someone I loved and I killed myself. She gave me power in a way. I could deal with anything now. She was not around. I still wish she is the happiest she can be. I hope if we meet someday, we can talk about everything like we never could but I would not counting on it. I will always be a villain for her. I hope I didn't leave her the same way I found her; On a flight with a sad face and strong eyes.

I woke up to a message from Sameera in my snapchat. Someone went lingerie shopping. Nothing beats good lingerie on a hot body. Except no lingerie on a hot body. Makes my worries go away but it still isn't anywhere near waking up next to her with her hands running through my hair. It is a vicious circle, isn't it? Falling in love. You fall in love, you get your heart broken enough to not love the people who actually love you. Then you break their hearts. Then they regift the gift to someone else. Meera was heartbroken when I met her. So was I. I put my problems on the side for so long that I had breakdown. It didn't workout. So, I should move on right? That's the smart thing to do. Somehow, in my life I never did the smart thing whenever given the option. I fucking love that. When I look back at it, I was the man that I was always meant to be. Following my gut and doing the right thing one step at a time. Meera once told me she wanted the old Abeer back. I was back to that but she was not around to see it. My family were more heartbroken than I could possibly be. They had seen me at my happiest around her. In some time I found out that I was happier because Meera gave me the courage to be myself. Years of wandering on trips, talking to strangers and doing the "right" thing I found myself at cross roads; Both roads had led to misery in the past. Currently, there was a pain of Meera's absence but not of life itself. Life was much more beautiful when I chose to do what I wanted instead of what was right. In turn my family was happier too. My friends were a delight as always. It's weird how I had so much going on when I was moving and yet nothing at all when I stood still. It took me a while to get over the reaction to my medication. In that period I did things I am not proud of. Borderline ashamed to be honest. I made mistakes beyond my own comprehension. I said things I didn't mean and did not say the things I wanted to. Meera was in the past. I was where I started my journey. I was not alright but I was another step closer.

As soon as I boarded the flight, I tried to look away from all the cabin crew. Spare myself all the drama of trying to find Meera on a flight. Anyway, She flies domestic. Although, she had been trying to fly international for a long time. I wonder if I she ever got in. On my window seat, I could see Delhi in all it's beauty. I fucking love this city. There was a girl sitting next to me who seemed a bit older than me. She was also taller than me. She had this strong face and beautiful smile. She was having whiskey, too. Damn, I love women who drink single malt. She was wearing those art hoe glasses, she was reading a book about Vincent Van Gogh on her phone. She smelled a lot like cigarettes. I was listening to The Weekend on mine. So, I took out a novel from my bag. Post office by Bukowski. That man is a sooth sayer. Then she took out the same book from her purse. Smiled at me. I raised my eyebrows. I notice I do that whenever I am intrigued by something.

"Damn. There's that itch again. An itch you gotta scratch." I told myself.

"I think you're on the wrong seat." I told her.

"What makes you think that?" She seemed amused.

"I know my luck. It ain't this good." I smiled.

The middle aged man sitting next to her was judging me hard. I loved it. She laughed. I loved that more. I stole that shit from Zakir Khan.

"You have some interesting tattoos. I see a Bukowski quote." She told me. "What does the lonely semicolon mean?"

I was just happy she recognised a quote by Bukowski.

"You can google it later. It's a cult tattoo." I told her.

She was silent for a while. So was I. We looked at each other. She smelled like coconut oil. I smelled like cigarettes. I don't know which one is better.

"So, what's your name?" I asked her.

"Akanksha."

That was a nice name.

"I looked at her and noticed that she was smiling at me."

"What?" I asked her.

"You don't remember me?"

I was silent. Should I remember her?

"Social, Odeon. You were drinking alone all sad. Was that you?" She asked.

"Probably." Yeah. That was a phase. In my defence my office is right next to Connaught Place.

I was about to say something when a chill ran down my spine. I felt uneasy beyond comprehension. My gut hurt and I could feel my heart trying to punch out of my chest. Something was wrong. I looked down the aisle. They were preparing to take off. The bathroom door opened. There was Meera again. Working as diligently as ever. Her hair grew back after the bad haircut she accidentally got. She looked fine to the layman but no one could ever tell. I knew she wasn't. Not related to me to be honest. I bet I was the last thing on her mind. In the moment I saw her, everything came rushing back. I thought my time with her was complicated and the love I had for her was based on happiness. Now, when I saw her I remembered every moment at once. Every time we snuggled up, every trip, every bad joke, every time I kissed her, every time I said the right things and especially every time I said the wrong ones. I had missed her beyond my own comprehension. It had started to feel like another life my time with her. Looking at her, reminded me of the reality of it. Meera and I did not have an adventure or an affair. You know when we think about love, we think how happy it was or how sad it could be. Love is not a single emotion. It's every emotion at once. It's a moment. Doesn't matter if your time together lasted a lifetime or just two days. If you truly love someone, it will always be a moment to you. A moment that went by too soon.

"Are you okay?" Akanksha asked.

"Yeah. Yeah. All good."

"You seem stressed."

"Yeah. Just wondering." I took a sip of my coffee.

"Wondering what?"

The last few times we talked, she had so much hatred for me in her voice. I had deeply hurt her. How do I show her my face again? I just hope I am in the section of the flight she's not going to attend tonight. It's a 6 hour flight. I could manage being in her blindspot, maybe. That was the practical thing to do. That's the weird thing about love. You can never tell what is the right path to follow. Every part of me would want her in my life but not at the cost of her happiness.

"Should I stay or should I go?" I whispered to myself.